Photographs
Photographs in Social Studies

Have you heard the phrase "One picture is worth a thousand words"? Look at the front page of the newspaper. What is the first thing that catches your attention? Most people look at newspaper photographs and headlines before reading the article. We live in a world full of visual images.

The GED Social Studies test will ask you to answer questions based on photographs or pictures. Picture interpretation skills are a new addition to the 2002 Series GED tests. Photographs are used either alone or in combination with a short passage. When using a photograph to answer GED questions, always read the title, caption, or other text that accompanies the photograph before choosing the answer.

Try this GED example. Choose the <u>one best answer</u> to the question. Then check your answer.

Composite photograph showing Los Angeles, California on a clear day (March 2) and on a day with dense smog (March 31).

1. Which of the following conclusions can be drawn from the photograph?

   (1) Smog-causing pollution has been reduced throughout the United States.
   (2) Smog is worse during the months of January and February than it is in the month of March.
   (3) The later in the month, the more likely Los Angeles will experience smog-free days.
   (4) The density of smog can differ from day to day.
   (5) Smog is prevalent only in large cities, such as Los Angeles.

1. **(4)** The smog levels vary on the two different days shown in the photograph. While option (1) may be true, it is not supported by the photograph. The photograph does not indicate that smog is impacted by the months of the year or days within a given month (options 2 and 3). Option (5) is not supported by information in the photograph.

Directions: Choose the <u>one best answer</u> to each question. <u>Questions 1 and 2</u> refer to the following photograph.

Directions: Choose the <u>one best answer</u> to each question. <u>Questions 3 and 4</u> refer to the following photograph.

The New Workforce

Washington: The Rev. Martin Luther King Jr. delivers his address at the Lincoln Memorial on August 28, 1963, during the civil rights march on Washington.

1. Which of the following statements does the photograph best support?

   (1) Women with children must work in order to maintain a middle class lifestyle.
   (2) A major social issue in today's workforce is balancing a career with family.
   (3) Women are happier being part of the workforce than raising families.
   (4) Today's workforce has not changed since World War II when many women held industrial jobs.
   (5) Most women today are employed in managerial or factory positions.

2. Many businesses find it more economically beneficial to maintain veteran employees than to recruit and train new ones. Based on this information and the photograph, which of the following best illustrates a company's commitment to its employees?

   (1) providing onsite daycare
   (2) restricting family leave to increase wages
   (3) requiring more overtime
   (4) increasing insurance costs to improve family coverage
   (5) providing mentors for female employees

3. In his "I Have a Dream" speech on August 28, King focused on the need for respect and understanding of the diversity of people living in the United States. He emphasized bringing about change through nonviolent protest. Which of following would most accurately reflect King's belief regarding the passage of civil rights legislation?

   (1) Civil rights legislation could only result from public unrest that threatened to become violent if not addressed.
   (2) Civil rights legislation could only result from a combination of understanding among diverse cultures and peaceful demonstrations.
   (3) Civil rights legislation could only result from the overthrow of the existing governmental structure.
   (4) Civil rights legislation could only occur if more than 50% of those voting were African Americans.
   (5) Civil rights legislation would be impossible during his lifetime.

Interpreting Visual Information

To the Learner 2

PHOTOGRAPHS AND EDITORIAL CARTOONS

Lesson 1 Photographs in Social Studies 3
GED Practice: Photographs in Social Studies 4

Lesson 2 Editorial Cartoons in Social Studies 6
GED Practice: Editorial Cartoons in Social Studies 7

TABLES AND CHARTS

Lesson 3 Tables and Charts in Social Studies and Science 9
GED Practice: Tables and Charts in Social Studies and Science 10

Lesson 4 Tables and Charts in Mathematics 12
GED Practice: Tables and Charts in Mathematics 13

GRAPHS

Lesson 5 Bar Graphs in Social Studies and Science 15
GED Practice: Bar Graphs in Social Studies and Science 16

Lesson 6 Bar Graphs in Mathematics 18
GED Practice: Bar Graphs in Mathematics 19

Lesson 7 Line Graphs in Social Studies and Science 21
GED Practice: Line Graphs in Social Studies and Science 22

Lesson 8 Line Graphs in Mathematics 24
GED Practice: Line Graphs in Mathematics 25

Lesson 9 Circle Graphs in Social Studies and Science 27
GED Practice: Circle Graphs in Social Studies and Science 28

Lesson 10 Circle Graphs in Mathematics 30
GED Practice: Circle Graphs in Mathematics 31

Lesson 11 Pictographs in Social Studies, Science, and Mathematics 33
GED Practice: Pictographs in Social Studies, Science, and Mathematics . . 34

DRAWINGS AND DIAGRAMS

Lesson 12 Drawings and Diagrams in Social Studies 36
GED Practice: Drawings and Diagrams in Social Studies 37

Lesson 13 Drawings and Diagrams in Science 39
GED Practice: Drawings and Diagrams in Science 40

MAPS

Lesson 14 Maps in Social Studies 42
GED Practice: Maps in Social Studies 43

Lesson 15 Maps in Science 45
GED Practice: Maps in Science 46

Answer Key 48

To the Learner

The *Steck-Vaughn GED Skill Books* are designed to give you practice in key areas stressed on the actual GED test. These books can be used alone or to supplement *Steck-Vaughn GED* books, *Steck-Vaughn Complete GED Preparation*, *Steck-Vaughn GED Exercise Books*, or any other GED preparation materials. The series consists of these books:

Language Arts, Writing: Mechanics and Usage
Language Arts, Writing: Sentence Structure and Organization
Language Arts, Writing: The Essay
Social Studies: U.S. History, World History, and Geography
Social Studies: Key Historical Documents
Social Studies: Economics, Civics and Government
Science: Life Science
Science: Physical Science, Earth and Space Science
Language Arts, Reading: Literary Texts
Language Arts, Reading: Nonfiction Texts
Mathematics: Number Operations and Algebra
Mathematics: Data Analysis, Statistics, Measurement, and Geometry
Mathematics: Calculator
Interpreting Visual Information
Higher Order Thinking Skills
Diagnostic Test: Full-Length Test
Evaluative Test: Full-Length Test

Interpreting Visual Information

This book will help you prepare for the questions on the GED Science, Social Studies, and Mathematics tests that contain information presented in visual, or graphic, form. The 15 lessons each address a specific type of graphic. Each lesson contains a **Skill Page** and a **GED Practice.**

- The **Skill Page** briefly reviews a skill and presents one or two practice GED questions with complete answers and explanations. Use this page to check your understanding of the skill. If you have trouble answering the questions on this page, talk to your instructor before continuing with the GED Practice.

- The two-page **GED Practice** provides an opportunity for you to practice answering questions that contain graphics like those on the actual GED test. Answers to the questions are on the back cover of this book. The practice pages also contain a number of tips you can use to help you prepare for and pass the GED test.

Staff Credits

Executive Editor
Ellen Northcutt
Senior Editor
Donna Townsend
Designers
Jessica Bristow
Rusty Kaim
Electronic Production Artist
Kimberly Reiley

ISBN: 0-7398-5747-9

4. What freedom is King exercising in the photograph?

(1) freedom of religion
(2) freedom of the press
(3) freedom from unreasonable search and seizure
(4) freedom of speech
(5) freedom to vote in national elections

Questions 5 and 6 refer to the following photograph.

President Roosevelt signs the declaration of war against Japan.

5. By declaring war against Japan, which of the following American policies related to the U.S. involvement in World War II did Roosevelt change?

(1) Truman Doctrine
(2) immigration laws
(3) isolationism
(4) military benefits
(5) financial support for education

6. Which of the following had an immediate impact on the American economy as a result of the declaration of war on Japan?

(1) increased military costs
(2) decreased military costs
(3) increased housing costs
(4) increased education costs
(5) decreased education costs

Question 7 refers to the following photograph.

A group of West Germans peer over the infamous Berlin Wall.

7. For more than 50 years, the Berlin Wall separated East Berlin from West Berlin. What did the Berlin Wall symbolize to the world?

(1) communism versus freedom
(2) acceptance of cultural diversity
(3) the end of World War II
(4) opening of communist countries to free trade
(5) open-door relations among nations

Tip

When you answer questions based on photographs, first identify the subject of the photograph. Sometimes photos capture a specific point in time. Having knowledge of the historic context and significance of the picture is helpful. Some questions on the GED test will require you to call upon your prior knowledge of the subject to answer the question.

Editorial Cartoons
Editorial Cartoons in Social Studies

Most people have opinions about current events and social changes. Many of these ideas are reflected through the editorial cartoons of the day. When people turn to the editorial page, a cartoon is often the first thing they see. These cartoons are a social or political commentary on the events of the world.

The GED test will ask you to answer questions based on editorial cartoons. These questions require that you be able to distinguish fact from opinion, identify symbolism, understand irony, and have a basic knowledge of the context surrounding the cartoon. Editorial cartoons are part of the time in which they are written. Basic historical knowledge can be helpful in understanding the cartoonist's point of view.

Try this GED example. Choose the <u>one best answer</u> to each question. Then check your answers.

1. What does the cartoonist assume readers understand about the subject of the cartoon?

   (1) the increasing number of senior citizens on a fixed income
   (2) the irony of senior citizens in today's technological world
   (3) the comparison of the space program to prescription drugs
   (4) the history of the development of prescription drugs
   (5) the necessity for grandparents to babysit their grandchildren

2. Which of the following best states the main idea of the cartoon?

   (1) Grandparents need to spend more quality time with their grandchildren.
   (2) The space program has drastically decreased the number of launches.
   (3) The availability of quality prescription drugs is rapidly decreasing.
   (4) The cost of prescription drugs needs to increase to cover the cost of research.
   (5) The cost of prescription drugs is rapidly increasing.

1. **(1)** The cartoonist assumes that individuals are aware of the increasing number of senior citizens who must live on a fixed income, making the rapid rise in the price of prescription drugs a hardship on them. Options (2), (3), (4), and (5) are incorrect. Faulty conclusions are provided in these choices that are not necessary to understanding the meaning of the cartoon.

2. **(5)** The cartoonist shows Grandpa watching the cost of drugs rise fast, like a rocket. Options (1), (2), (3), and (4) express points of view that are not the focus of the cartoon.

Directions: Choose the one best answer to each question. Questions 1 and 2 refer to the following cartoon.

1. What is the cartoonist's message?

   (1) Staff must clean up after elections.
   (2) The workers, not the elected officials, compile campaign promises.
   (3) Elections promote ideas that are not acted upon following an election.
   (4) Those who are hired following an election keep campaign promises.
   (5) Politicians purposely tell lies in order to win elections.

2. What does the figure in the cartoon represent?

   (1) the American public
   (2) custodial workers
   (3) politicians
   (4) world leaders
   (5) bureaucrats

Tip

To analyze an editorial cartoon, ask:
- What event or issue inspired the cartoon?
- Who is portrayed in the cartoon? Are they real people?
- Are there symbols in the cartoon? What are they and what do they represent?
- What opinion or attitude does the cartoonist reveal in the cartoon?

Questions 3 and 4 refer to the following cartoon.

3. Since the fall of communism in Russia, there have been various changes in that country's leadership. Which of the following is a conclusion that the cartoonist wanted the readers to draw?

   (1) Yeltsin was a poor leader who was forced out of office in 2001.
   (2) Putin faced many economic and political problems when he became Russia's new leader.
   (3) Russia gained new leadership through a hostile take-over.
   (4) The fall of communism caused all of Russia's economic problems.
   (5) Russia is a major force in world affairs.

4. What does the bear in the cartoon represent?

   (1) a hostile take-over
   (2) a means of transportation
   (3) a peace-offering
   (4) economic and political problems
   (5) political control

5. During 2001, Wen Ho Lee, a scientist of Chinese decent who worked at the Los Alamos National Laboratory, was arrested and held for almost a year due to allegations that he had copied classified documents. What does the cartoonist assume readers understand about the subject of the cartoon?

   (1) During World War II, many Japanese-American citizens were detained in interment camps.
   (2) Wen Ho Lee was detained in the same relocation camp used during World War II for Japanese-Americans.
   (3) Japanese-Americans were detained in relocation camps for copying classified documents.
   (4) Wen Ho Lee's First Amendment rights were violated.
   (5) During wartime, the right to a fair and speedy trial is abolished.

6. What does the padlocked door in the cartoon represent?

   (1) protection against terrorism
   (2) implementation of states' rights as enumerated in the Tenth Amendment
   (3) institution of excessive bail as defined by the Eight Amendment
   (4) violation of Fifth Amendment Rights of life, liberty, and due process
   (5) the isolation of Wen Ho Lee from the relocation camp

7. What irony does the cartoonist imply by the drawing?

   (1) The United States' treatment of Asian Americans has not changed since World War II.
   (2) The United States no longer uses unlawful interment.
   (3) The Japanese-American relocation camps of the 1940s and the present day solitary confinement of Wen Ho Lee are not the same.
   (4) The United States does not accept foreign-born individuals.
   (5) Only Asian Americans are held in violation of constitutional rights.

Question 8 refers to the following cartoon.

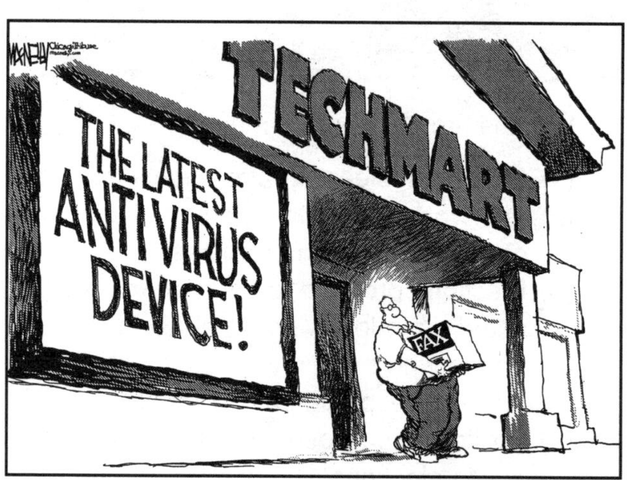

8. What is the implication of the cartoon?

   (1) Using telephones is safer than using computers.
   (2) The latest antivirus software is called Fax.
   (3) Technology continues to improve.
   (4) Technology is outdated before a person can walk out of a store.
   (5) Viruses are no longer a problem for computers.

Tables and Charts

Tables and Charts in Social Studies and Science

Graphics, like words, convey information, but in visual form. The GED Social Studies and Science tests use graphics on 50–60% of test questions. Some questions will ask you to use information from charts and tables. Charts and tables organize information in rows and columns. Items of data are found where the columns and rows meet. To locate a specific piece of data, use column headings as your beginning point. Then scan down the column until you locate the row that identifies the information you need.

Try this GED example. Choose the one best answer to each question. Then check your answers.

The four major blood groups are A, B, AB, and O. Blood groups are defined by the presence of antigens and antibodies in blood plasma. Red blood cells have unique antigens, or proteins, that give blood cells their identity. A gene determines the particular antigen displayed by a red blood cell, and this gene has three alleles, or forms: A, B, and O. Plasma also contains antibodies, or proteins produced by the body to destroy "not-self," or foreign antigens. A person's blood type determines which antibodies exist in the plasma, meaning, for example, that a person with Type A blood carries the A antigen and B antibodies. Antibodies contribute to the rejection of mismatched blood during transfusions and organ transplants.

Blood Types				
Blood Type	Antigen		Antibody	
	A	B	anti-A	anti-B
A	+	−	−	+
B	−	+	+	−
O	−	−	+	+
AB	+	+	−	−

(+) indicates protein's presence
(−) indicates protein's absence

1. Based on the passage and the table, which of the following statements is true?

   (1) People who have Type AB blood have A and B antibodies.
   (2) People with the B antigen do not have B antibodies.
   (3) People with the A antigen have both A and B antibodies.
   (4) People who have neither the A nor the B antigen have neither A nor B antibodies.
   (5) People with the A and B antigens have A and B antibodies.

2. If someone with an unknown blood type requires a transfusion, what blood type would be the safest?

   (1) Type A
   (2) Type B
   (3) Type O
   (4) Type AB
   (5) any blood type

---

1. (2) According to the chart, type B blood has a + in the B antigen column and a − in the B antibody column. Neither the table nor the passage contains information to support options (1), (3), (4), or (5).

2. (3) According to the chart, type O blood does not have A and B antigens. The passage states that antibodies destroy foreign antigens. If a person were to receive blood with foreign antigens, antibodies in the person's body would destroy the antigens. Only type O blood has no antigens. Options (1), (2), and (4) have antigens. Option (5) includes blood with antigens.

Tables and Charts in Social Studies and Science

Directions: Choose the one best answer to each question. Questions 1 through 3 refer to the following table.

State Budget Cuts and Additions	
Public Schools	− $250.3 million
Criminal Justice Systems	− $125.2 million
Community Colleges	− $ 30.8 million
State University System	− $ 78.2 million
Transportation	− $ 29.2 million
Scholarships	− $ 8.1 million
Substance Abuse Treatment Program	− $ 3.4 million
Welfare-to-Work Training	+ $ 8.9 million
Tourism Promotion	+ $ 27.2 million
Highway Construction	+ $328.1 million
School Construction	+ $223.1 million
Security	+ $ 28.7 million
Tax Incentives	+ $428.3 million

1. Which of the following statements is the best summary of the information in the table?

   (1) The state financially supports and values education.
   (2) The state previously over funded the education system.
   (3) Funding favors the elderly.
   (4) Funding favors areas that produce revenue rather than those that provide a public service.
   (5) The state's road system requires extensive repair.

2. What is most likely to happen to education if the system is currently using all funding provided?

   (1) The state will no longer be able to build schools.
   (2) Schools in some areas of the state will close.
   (3) The state will not be able to cut the education budgets.
   (4) Schools will not be able to operate.
   (5) Classes may be larger and programs may have to be deleted.

3. Which of the following conclusions can be drawn from the information in the table?

   (1) The state is attempting to jump-start its economy.
   (2) The state is not attempting to balance the budget.
   (3) The state has a progressive educational system.
   (4) The state is levying additional taxes.
   (5) The state is cutting funding to all programs.

Questions 4 through 6 refer to the following passage and chart.

Taxonomy is the branch of science that develops the rules for naming, describing, and classifying organisms into different categories. The biological sciences use a classification system invented by Carolus Linnaeus. The Linnaean classification system organizes all living things according to a prescribed hierarchy. Biologists classify organisms into the different categories by assessing the similarities and differences of each sample—the more similarities that exist, the closer the biological relationship of the organisms.

Classification of Living Things in the Linnaean System			
Kingdom	Structure	Nutrition	Types of Organisms
Monera	Simple, single-celled organism	Absorb food	Bacteria, blue-green algae, spirochetes
Protista	Large, single-celled organism	Absorb, ingest, or photo-synthesize food	Protozoans and algae
Fungi	Multicellular organism	Absorb food	Funguses, molds, mushrooms, yeasts, mildews, smuts
Plantae	Multicellular organism	Photo-synthesize food	Mosses, ferns, non-flowering, and flowering plants
Animalia	Multicellular organism	Ingest food	Sponges, worms, insects, fish, birds, amphibians, reptiles, mammals

4. Which of the following conclusions is supported by the information in the passage and the chart?

   (1) A kingdom is a large division within the Linnaean Classification system.
   (2) Some living things cannot be classified into the Linnaean system.
   (3) All species of living things have been identified.
   (4) Organisms are classified by their color.
   (5) The Linnaean Classification system organizes living and non-living organisms.

5. According to the chart, with which of the following do mammals share the most similarities?

   (1) protozoans
   (2) monera
   (3) plantae
   (4) amphibians
   (5) funguses

6. How do ferns, mosses, and non-flowering plants obtain their nutrition?

   (1) by absorbing food from the environment
   (2) by ingesting nutrients from the ground
   (3) by synthesizing energy from the sun to create carbohydrates
   (4) by ingesting air-borne food particles
   (5) by absorbing, ingesting, or photosynthesizing food

Tip

Chart means any visual display of information. Table is often, but not always, used to refer to a chart with data displayed in rows and columns. Sometimes table is even more narrowly defined to mean a chart of numerical data arranged in rows and columns—for example, a tax table. In general all tables are charts, but not all charts are tables.

Question 7 refers to the following chart and passage.

The Feudal System of the Middle Ages	
Position	**Duties**
King	Protected the people under his domain Provided land to the nobles
Nobles	Paid taxes to the king Ruled the land given to them by the king Protected those living within the manors Provided homes to the peasants
Knights	Fought to protect the king and nobles
Peasants	Lived within the manors Were poor people who worked for the nobles Paid taxes to the nobles

The division of Europe into many different kingdoms during the Middle Ages resulted in a system called feudalism. After the fall of the Roman Empire, barbarians invaded Europe, and many of the cities were destroyed. Feudalism provided a way to protect lands and the people who lived there. Feudalism in Europe lasted for over 700 years.

7. What conclusion about feudalism can be drawn from the information in the chart and passage?

   (1) In the feudal system, peasants were often given land by the king.
   (2) Feudalism adopted an enlightened attitude about education and government.
   (3) The feudal system was based on democratic concepts where each individual was free to aspire to a chosen position.
   (4) Nobles often worked the fields alongside the peasants.
   (5) Peasants were the largest group in the feudal system due to the need for cheap labor to operate the manors.

Tables and Charts

Tables and Charts in Mathematics

Tables and charts help make sense of information. Instead of providing a list of numbers or facts, tables and charts arrange information into columns and rows. Newspapers use tables and charts so that the reader can quickly find information. Baseball statistics, labor market trends, and stock market gains or losses are often shown in tables or charts.

The GED Mathematics test will require you to use charts and tables to answer questions. Read the title of the chart or table. Next, read the headings and subheadings before looking at the data in the body of the table. Look for patterns or the lack of patterns in the data and determine how the totals or subtotals are calculated.

Try this GED example. Choose the <u>one best answer</u> to each question. Then check your answers.

Bus Schedule			
Newton to Lehigh			
City	Miles	Bus #1 Daily	Bus #2 Daily
Newton	0	7:10 A.M.	5:00 P.M.
Monticello	40	8:08 A.M.	6:08 P.M.
Greenwood	82	9:22 A.M.	7:28 P.M.
Hazelton	130	10:36 A.M.	8:50 P.M.
Easton	192	11:55 A.M.	10:15 P.M.
Harrisburg	303	2:39 P.M.	12:50 A.M.
Lehigh	452	5:08 P.M.	1:07 A.M.

1. How long does it take Bus #1 to travel from Monticello to Harrisburg?

   (1) 5 hours, 69 minutes
   (2) 6 hours, 9 minutes
   (3) 6 hours, 31 minutes
   (4) 6 hours, 44 minutes
   (5) 6 hours, 42 minutes

2. How many miles per hour does Bus #2 average for a full one-way trip?

   (1) 40
   (2) 452
   (3) 5.82
   (4) 55.69
   (5) 56.01

1. **(3)** Find the column for Bus #1 and the row for Monticello. The square where the row and column intersect shows the time the bus leaves Monticello. Next find the square where Harrisburg and Bus #1 intersect, which shows the time the bus arrives in Harrisburg. To arrive at the correct answer, remember that an hour has 60 minutes, not 100. Options (1) and (2) use incorrect formulas to subtract time. Options (4) and (5) use data from the Bus #2 column rather than Bus #1.

2. **(4)** Locate the number of miles traveled for a one-way trip by going to the end of the second column. Then figure how many hours the bus spends on the road. Change the time into a fraction or decimal since an hour has sixty minutes. From 5:00 P.M. until 1:07 A.M. becomes 8 hours and 7 minutes. Change the 7 minutes into a decimal form, 0.11667. Now divide the number of miles (452) by the decimal equivalent of hours (8.11667). Options (1) and (2) report the number of miles between specific distances. Option (3) reports the average number of miles per hour traveled by Bus #1. Option (5) mistakenly uses 8.07 as the number of hours (7 minutes of an hour does not equal 7/100).

Tables and Charts in Mathematics

Directions: Choose the <u>one best answer</u> to each question. Questions 1 through 3 refer to the following table.

Employee Salaries at the Ellis Manufacturing Company		
Number of Employees	**Position**	**Salary**
25	On-line workers	$21,000
8	Skilled professional workers	$28,900
6	Supervisors	$34,600
4	Clerical support staff	$16,400
2	Managers	$48,600
1	CEO	$78,000

1. To the nearest whole number, what is the mean of the salaries offered by the company?

   (1) $21,000
   (2) $24,760
   (3) $27,500
   (4) $31,750
   (5) $37,917

2. According to the table, approximately what percentage of employees at the company makes less than $30,000 per year?

   (1) 50%
   (2) 66%
   (3) 80%
   (4) 87%
   (5) 91%

3. What is the total amount Ellis Manufacturing Company pays annually in salary?

   (1) $ 227,500
   (2) $ 298,300
   (3) $ 556,000
   (4) $ 902,600
   (5) $1,204,600

Question 4 refers to the following tables.

4. Janice and Elise each conducted a survey of people's favorite colors. Both surveyed 65 people and asked them each to select a favorite color. The results of the two surveys are depicted in the tables below.

Janice's Survey Results	
Color	Percent
Red	40%
Blue	25%
Purple	17%
Green	8%
Orange	6%
Yellow	4%

Elise's Survey Results	
Color	Number
Red	26
Blue	15
Purple	10
Green	9
Orange	3
Yellow	2

Based on the tables, which of the following statements is true?

   (1) The results of both surveys are the same.
   (2) Twenty-six people selected red as their favorite color in both surveys.
   (3) Ten people selected purple as their favorite color in both surveys.
   (4) Two people selected yellow as their favorite color in both surveys.
   (5) There are no statistical similarities in the two surveys.

Question 5 refers to the following chart.

x	y
1	3
2	5
3	7
4	9

5. According to the chart, which of the following expressions could be used to find the value of y?

   (1) $x + 1$
   (2) $2x + 1$
   (3) $1 - 2x$
   (4) $3x - 1$
   (5) $1 - 3x$

Questions 6 through 8 refer to the following table.

Temperatures for Selected Southern Cities

City	Today's Forecast		Yesterday	
	High	Low	High	Low
Atlanta	60	42	68	51
Charleston	66	46	80	52
Charlotte	58	41	74	52
Jackson	50	36	69	57
Louisville	42	29	65	50
Memphis	49	30	67	51
Nashville	47	35	62	51
Orlando	79	62	83	64
New Orleans	56	45	76	59

6. According to the table, where will freezing temperatures likely occur today?

   (1) Jackson, Louisville, Memphis, and Nashville
   (2) Louisville, Memphis, and Nashville
   (3) Louisville and Memphis
   (4) Memphis only
   (5) Louisville only

7. According to the table, the widest variation in temperature occurred in which of these cities?

   (1) Charleston
   (2) Charlotte
   (3) Memphis only
   (4) Orlando only
   (5) New Orleans

8. Which city will likely experience the largest drop in high temperatures from yesterday to today?

   (1) Charleston
   (2) Charlotte
   (3) Jackson
   (4) Louisville
   (5) Memphis

Questions 9 and 10 refer to the following table.

Furniture and Shipping Costs

Cost of Furniture	$0 – $100	$100 – $250	$250 – $349.99	Over $350
Shipping Costs	$12.50	$23.75	$39.50	$47.25

9. Deidra purchased a chair for $149.95 and an end table for $119.75. What is the total cost of her order if shipped as a single order?

   (1) $173.70
   (2) $269.70
   (3) $309.20
   (4) $316.95
   (5) $317.20

10. What is the total price, including shipping, that a customer will pay for a piece of furniture that costs $398.25?

    (1) $ 47.25
    (2) $397.25
    (3) $398.25
    (4) $445.50
    (5) $453.25

Tables and charts often contain more information than is needed to answer a question. Always identify what specific information is needed to answer the question. Carefully read and understand the topic of the chart and the headings of the columns and rows. Identify where the necessary data is located by following the appropriate column and row to where they intersect.

Lesson 4

Graphs
Bar Graphs in Social Studies and Science

Bar graphs are one of the most common types of graphs used to compare data. A bar graph is built on a vertical and a horizontal axis. These axes are similar to the columns and rows in tables. A bar graph uses thick bars to represent data. These bars are drawn either vertically or horizontally. When reading a bar graph, determine what is represented by each bar and then compare the data by viewing the different lengths of each bar.

Bar graphs may use either single or multiple bars to display data. As with other types of graphics, you should read the title of the graph and the vertical and horizontal labels carefully. Bar graphs may also contain a legend and a scale to help you interpret the value of each bar.

The GED Social Studies and Science tests will ask you to answer questions based on the information contained in bar graphs. Some questions may present two or more graphs to compare or contrast.

Try this GED example. Choose the <u>one best answer</u> to each question. Then check your answers.

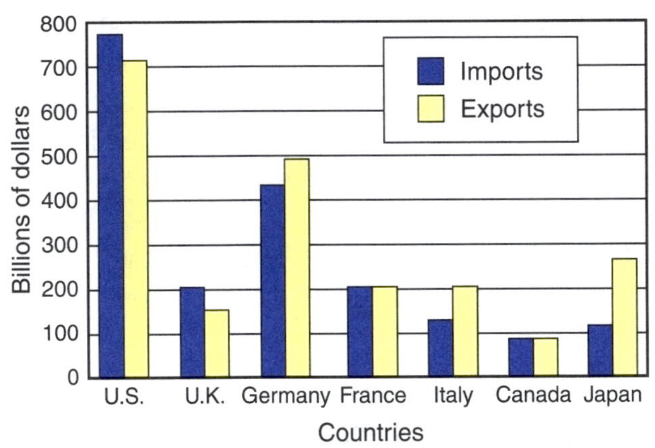

1. Which two nations have approximately the same value of exports?

    (1) U.K. and France
    (2) France and Canada
    (3) France and Italy
    (4) Italy and Japan
    (5) U.S. and Germany

2. Which nation has the greatest difference between the level of imports and exports?

    (1) U.S.
    (2) U.K.
    (3) Germany
    (4) Italy
    (5) Japan

3. Which of the following countries import more than they export?

    (1) Germany, Italy, and Japan
    (2) France and Canada
    (3) U.S. and U.K.
    (4) U.S. and Germany
    (5) Japan and Italy

---

1. **(3)** Both France and Italy export approximately 200 billion dollars worth of goods. Options (1) and (4) compare values in imports, not exports. Options (2) and (5) show nations that have different dollar values for exports.

2. **(5)** Japan exports over 100 billion dollars more in products than it imports. The difference between imports and exports is smaller in the U.S., U.K., Germany, and Italy (options 1, 2, 3, and 4).

3. **(3)** Both the U.S. and the U.K. import more than they export. The countries in options (1) and (5) all have more exports than imports. Option (2) shows countries in which exports and imports are equal. Option (4) shows one country that imports more and one country that exports more.

Bar Graphs in Social Studies and Science

<u>Directions</u>: Choose the <u>one best answer</u> to each question. <u>Questions 1 through 4</u> refer to the following passage and graph.

The environment is increasingly being recognized as a resource that cannot be replaced. Important to the well-being of the environment are all of the different species of animals and plants that live on land and in the water. Each year, more and more species are disappearing from Earth. Some species are endangered because of changes in the environment. These changes may be natural, but are more often brought about by human activity. With increasing population growth and industrialization, protecting all the different species on Earth is a growing cause of concern.

Endangered and Threatened Species

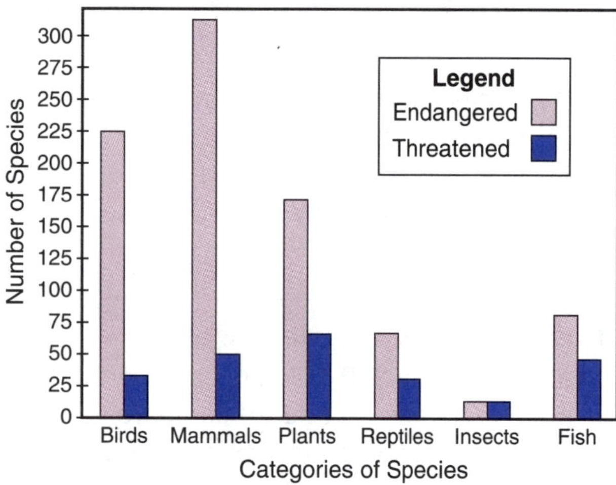

1. Based on the information in the passage and graph, what prediction could be made about threatened and endangered species?

   (1) Endangered and threatened species will continue towards extinction.
   (2) Mankind does not care about endangered and threatened species.
   (3) The number of endangered and threatened species will decrease in the future.
   (4) The extinction of certain species is due to natural causes.
   (5) Industrialization has been the primary cause of the extinction.

2. Which two categories show the least number of endangered species?

   (1) birds and insects
   (2) reptiles and insects
   (3) insects and fish
   (4) reptiles and fish
   (5) birds and fish

3. Which of the following conclusions is supported by the information in the passage and graph?

   (1) Insects are more resilient to the environment.
   (2) Industrialization is more threatening to birds than plant life.
   (3) Water pollution has decreased, thus causing a decrease in the number of endangered and threatened species of fish.
   (4) Environmental and manmade changes have resulted in an increasing number of endangered and threatened species.
   (5) Extinction of the different species is the result of natural selection.

4. Between which two categories is the number of endangered species most similar?

   (1) birds and mammals
   (2) birds and plants
   (3) mammals and plants
   (4) reptiles and fish
   (5) plants and fish

Tip

When studying bar graphs, ask:
- What is the subject of the graph?
- How do the various parts relate to the subject?
- What relative percentage does each bar represent?
- What is the starting point for each bar?
- What interval is being used to display the information?

Every human body has—and needs—blood pressure. Without it, blood can't circulate through the body and provide organs with the oxygen and food they need to function. Blood pressure is measured in millimeters of mercury (mm HG).

Knowing your blood pressure rate is important to a healthy lifestyle. Blood pressure is measured in ranges with optimal or normal blood pressure ranging from below 120 to approximately 139 mm HG. Hypertension, or high blood pressure, is measured in three different stages.

According to recent estimates, one in four U.S. adults has high blood pressure, but because there are often no symptoms, nearly one-third of these people are unaware that they have it. This is why high blood pressure is often called the "silent killer." Uncontrolled high blood pressure can lead to stroke, heart attack, congestive heart failure, or kidney failure. The only way to tell if you have high blood pressure is to have your blood pressured checked regularly.

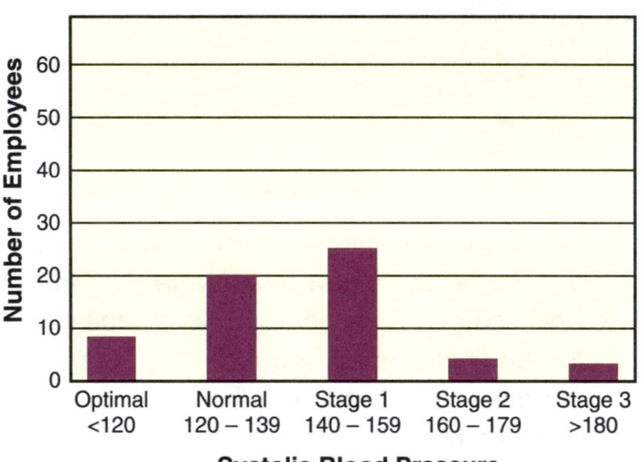

5. How many employees of Avid Software exhibit blood pressure in the hypertensive range?

    (1) 3 employees
    (2) 4 employees
    (3) 8 employees
    (4) 25 employees
    (5) 32 employees

6. Based on the information in the passage and the graph, which of the following conclusions could be made?

    (1) Positions at Avid Software are stressful, causing many employees to exhibit high blood pressure.
    (2) A larger percentage of employees at Avid Software have high blood pressure than the average U.S. population.
    (3) A less proportionate number of employees at Avid Software have high blood pressure than the average U.S. population.
    (4) All Avid Software Employees exhibit symptoms of high blood pressure.
    (5) None of the Avid Software Employees exhibit symptoms of high blood pressure.

U.S. Population Growth, 1790–1820

7. Based on the graph, which of the following statements is true?

    (1) The period of greatest growth was between 1795 and 1800.
    (2) The greatest increase in growth occurred during the early years of the period.
    (3) The U.S. population more than doubled between 1790 and 1820.
    (4) The U.S. population grew about 25% between 1790 and 1820.
    (5) The period of least growth was between 1810 and 1815.

Graphs
Bar Graphs in Mathematics

Bar graphs are used to compare and contrast numerical data in mathematics. Graphs are helpful because they can make complicated information easy to understand.

When using a bar graph to answer a mathematical question, first review the question to identify what type of information and calculation is required. Next familiarize yourself with the graph, reviewing the titles of the graph and the axes, as well as the starting point and scale of the axes. Remember to identify any keys or legends that are part of the graph. Use an appropriate problem-solving strategy to identify the correct answer and check back to the question and the graph to ensure that your answer is reasonable and answers the question.

Some GED Mathematics questions will ask you to identify specific information from bar graphs. Other questions will require that you use data from the graphs to complete a mathematical calculation.

Try this GED example. Choose the one best answer to each question. Then check your answers.

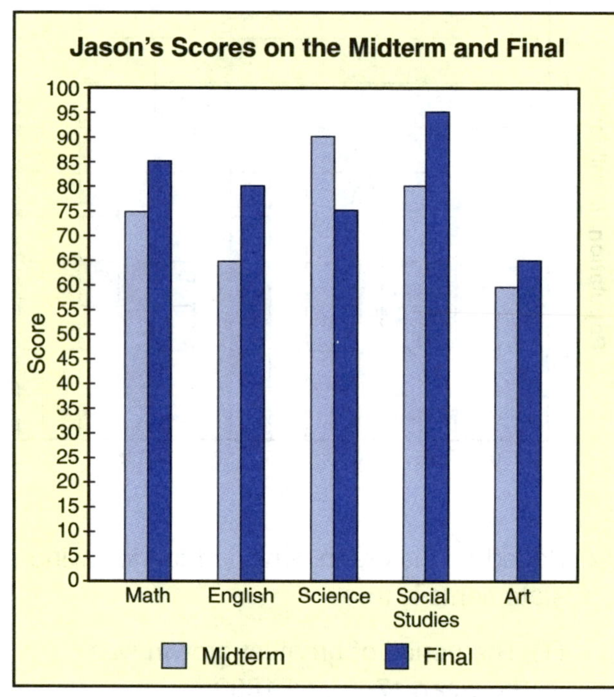

1. Based on the graph, what is the difference between the mean score of the midterms and the mean score of the finals?

   (1) 80
   (2) 75
   (3) 74
   (4) 6
   (5) 4

2. In which of the following areas did Jason show the greatest percentage of increase from his midterm to his final test?

   (1) Math
   (2) English
   (3) Science
   (4) Social Studies
   (5) Art

---

1. (4) Add all the midterm scores and divide by 5 to get the mean or average. Add the final scores and divide by 5 to get the mean for the finals. Finally, subtract the mean of the midterm scores from the mean of the final scores.

2. (2) To calculate the greatest percentage of increase, find the difference between the midterm and final score and divide it by the midterm score. Both English (option 2) and Social Studies (option 4) increased by 15 points. However, English showed the greatest percentage increase. Options (1), (3), and (5) showed either a decrease or an increase of less than 23%.

GED Skill Book • Interpreting Visual Information

Bar Graphs in Mathematics

Directions: Choose the <u>one best answer</u> to each question. Questions 1 through 4 refer to the following graph.

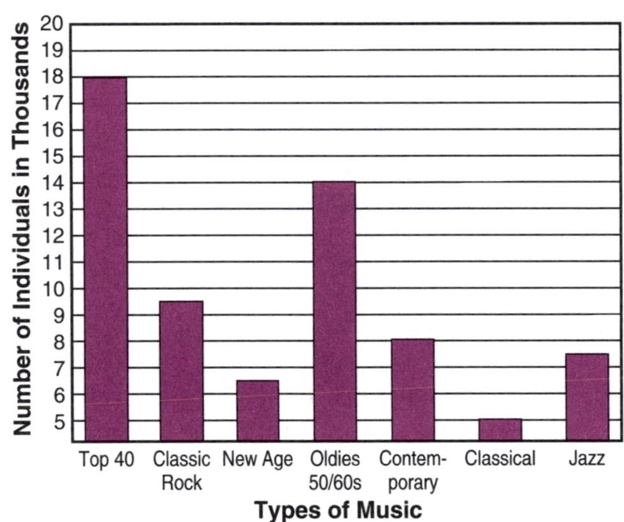

1. If the individuals surveyed could select only one choice, approximately how many people are represented in the graph?

   (1) 140,000
   (2) 68,500
   (3) 20,000
   (4) 685
   (5) 20

2. How many more of the individuals surveyed listen to Top 40 than to Contemporary music?

   (1) 26,000
   (2) 18,000
   (3) 10,000
   (4) 18
   (5) 10

3. Based on the survey, approximately what percentage of the individuals surveyed indicated that they preferred Classic Rock?

   (1) 0.7%
   (2) 7.2%
   (3) 14%
   (4) 33%
   (5) 72%

4. On the basis of the data in the graph, which of the following would be the best programming choice for the manager of the radio station?

   (1) Play primarily classical and jazz recordings to diversify the music offerings.
   (2) Play primarily songs recorded in the 50s and 60s due to the large number of individuals born in the 40s and 50s.
   (3) Play mainly Top 40 selections.
   (4) Play all types of music because of the diverse results of the survey.
   (5) Disregard the survey for the purpose of programming.

 **Tip**

Often the top of a bar on a bar graph does not line up with any label on the vertical axis. It falls between two labels. To estimate the value of such a bar, estimate how close it is to the higher label—halfway, one third, one fourth of the way, etc.

Next figure what number equates to that fraction of the distance between the two labeled numbers. For example, if a bar graph is divided into increments of 10 and the top bar is approximately one third of the way between the numbers 30 and 40, the reading would be 33.

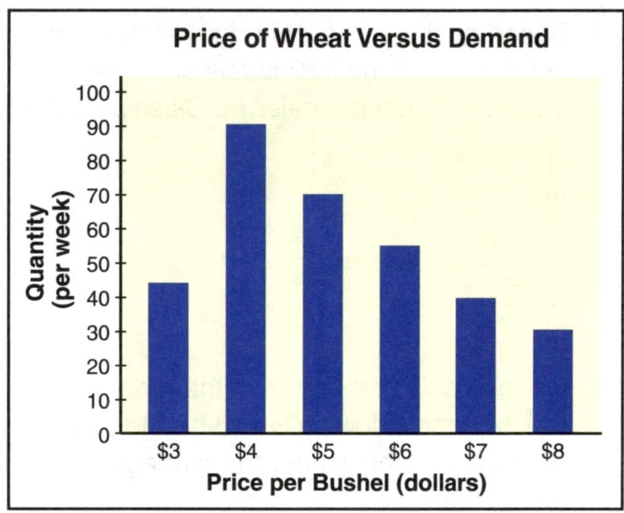

5. At what price per bushel was there the greatest demand for wheat?

   (1) $3
   (2) $4
   (3) $5
   (4) $6
   (5) $7

6. Approximately how many more bushels of wheat were sold at $4.00 per bushel than at $8.00 per bushel?

   (1) 30 bushels
   (2) 40 bushels
   (3) 60 bushels
   (4) 70 bushels
   (5) 90 bushels

7. Supply and demand is an important concept in the world of trade. Using the information on the graph and the concept of supply and demand, which price per bushel indicates the least optimal price of wheat per the demand for the product?

   (1) $3.00 per bushel
   (2) $4.00 per bushel
   (3) $6.00 per bushel
   (4) $7.00 per bushel
   (5) $8.00 per bushel

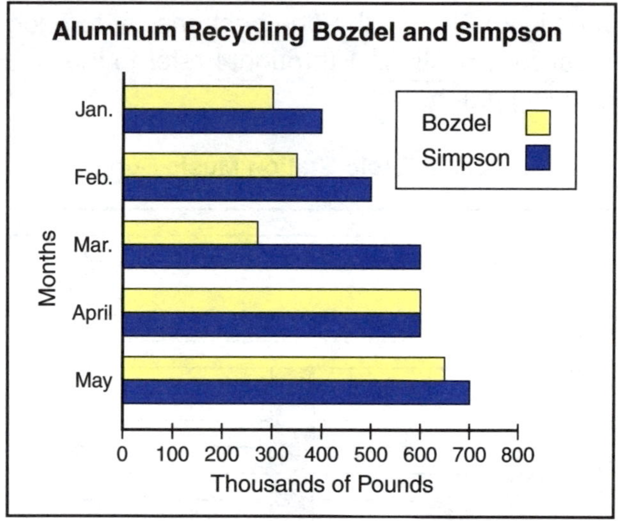

8. Approximately how many more pounds of aluminum did Simpson recycle in March than January?

   (1)   25
   (2)   200
   (3)   400
   (4)   600
   (5) 200,000

9. During which month did Bozdel show a decrease in recycling?

   (1) January
   (2) February
   (3) March
   (4) April
   (5) May

10. What was the percent of increase in recycling for Simpson from January to May?

   (1) 0.75%
   (2) 7.5%
   (3) 75%
   (4) 0.57%
   (5) 57%

Graphs
Line Graphs in Social Studies and Science

A line graph contains two parts: an *x*-axis, running across (horizontally), and a *y*-axis, running up and down (vertically). A line graph is used to display how one variable changes with respect to another variable. Line graphs display trend lines, often showing how the amount or number of something changes. To interpret information on line graphs, you must be able to locate specific points on the graphs and identify the trend that the graph represents.

Questions on the GED test will require you to analyze the information contained in a graph and identify reasons that could explain a specific trend.

Try this GED example. Choose the <u>one best answer</u> to each question. Then check your answers.

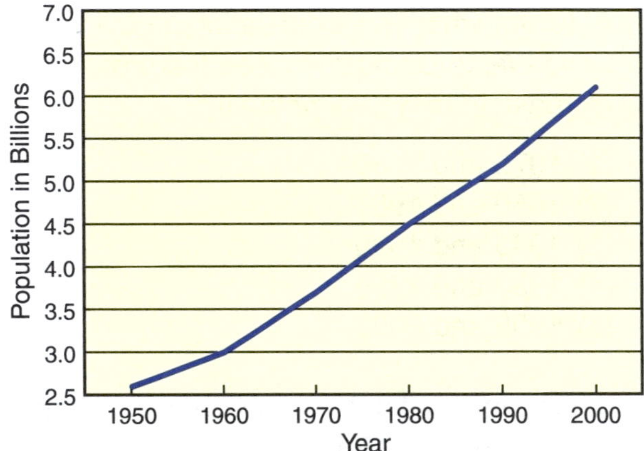

1. Many individuals are concerned about the rapid increase in the world's population and the ability of Earth to support the increased numbers. Using the trend of the past half century, what would be an approximate population projection for 2010?

   (1) 6.0 billion
   (2) 6.8 billion
   (3) 7.7 billion
   (4) 8.5 billion
   (5) 10.0 billion

2. Which of the following statements is supported by the information in the graph?

   (1) The world's rapid population growth has occurred primarily in third world countries.
   (2) The world's population has slowly increased over the past fifty years.
   (3) The world's population has remained static over the past fifty years.
   (4) The world's population has doubled since 1960.
   (5) The world's food supply will not be able to keep up with the rapid growth in population.

---

1. **(2)** Draw a line continuing the blue line on the graph. Move right along the *x*-axis to a point that matches the interval between decades. This would be the point for 2010. Draw a vertical line from this point to intersect the continuation of the blue line. Option (1) is a number less than the 2000 population. Options (3), (4), and (5) exceed the trend indicated on the graph.

2. **(4)** Only this option addresses facts that are supported by the graph—the doubling of the world's population since 1960. Options (1) and (5) draw conclusions not supported by the data. Options (2) and (3) contradict the data.

Directions: Choose the <u>one best answer</u> to the question. <u>Questions 1 and 2</u> refer to the following graph.

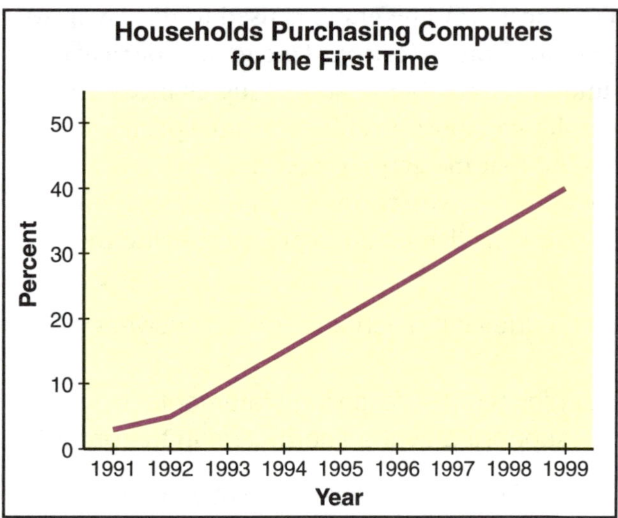

Questions 3 and 4 refer to the following graph.

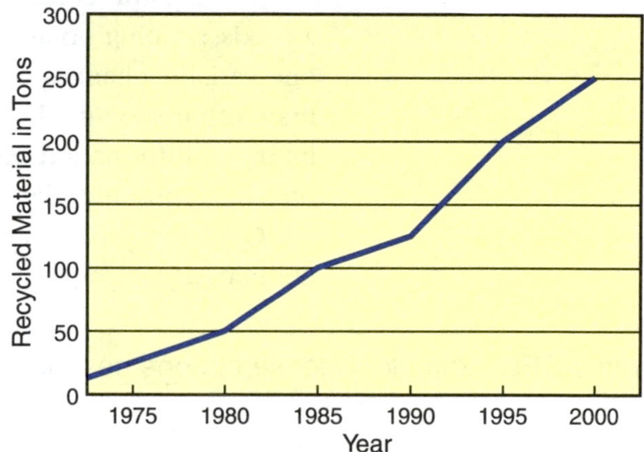

1. Which of the following statements is supported by information in the graph?

   (1) Since 1990 more than 50% of U.S. homes have purchased a computer.
   (2) The greatest increase in the number of computers purchased was between 1991 and 1992.
   (3) Nobody owned a personal computer before 1991.
   (4) In the 1990s, many people decided to replace old computers with newer ones.
   (5) The percent of households purchasing computers has steadily increased each year since 1991.

2. Which of the following would occur if the trend shown in the graph continues?

   The percentage of U.S. households owning computers will

   (1) increase for a year or two before decreasing
   (2) decrease for a year or two before increasing again
   (3) increase steadily
   (4) decrease steadily
   (5) peak at 40% and remain at 40% for the next 3 years

3. Between what years did Jefferson County Solid Waste Department see the greatest increase in recycled material?

   (1) 1975 and 1980
   (2) 1980 and 1985
   (3) 1985 and 1990
   (4) 1990 and 1995
   (5) 1995 and 2000

4. If recycling continues at the same rate that it has between 1995 and 2000, approximately how much recycled material will there be in 2005?

   (1) 250 tons
   (2) 300 tons
   (3) 350 tons
   (4) 400 tons
   (5) 450 tons

Tip

A line graph shows changes in amounts over time with an **indicator line,** which you always read from left to right.

Questions 5 through 7 refer to the following graph.

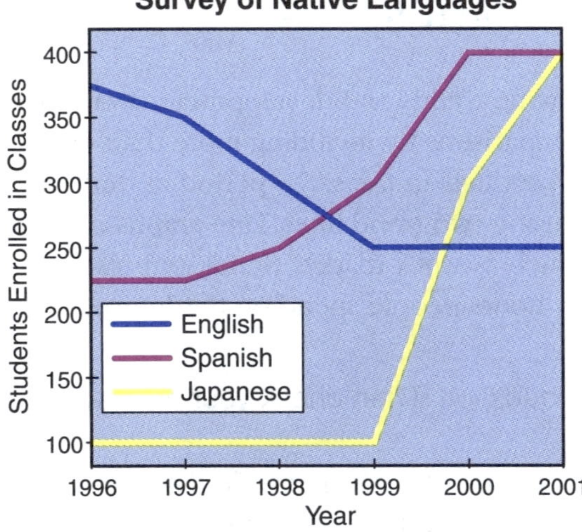

5. Which year saw the greatest increase in students whose native language was other than English?

    (1) 1996
    (2) 1997
    (3) 1998
    (4) 1999
    (5) 2000

6. During what two years did the school experience its sharpest decline in English-speaking students?

    (1) 1996—1998
    (2) 1997—1999
    (3) 1998—2000
    (4) 1999—2001
    (5) 2000—2002

7. Which of the following conclusions could you draw about enrollment at the center?

    (1) There are no English-speaking students enrolled.
    (2) Classes for non-native English speakers have increased significantly.
    (3) Unemployment rates have caused an increase in English-speaking students.
    (4) Enrollment at the local community college must have increased.
    (5) Classes for native English speakers have increased.

Questions 8 and 9 refer to the following graph.

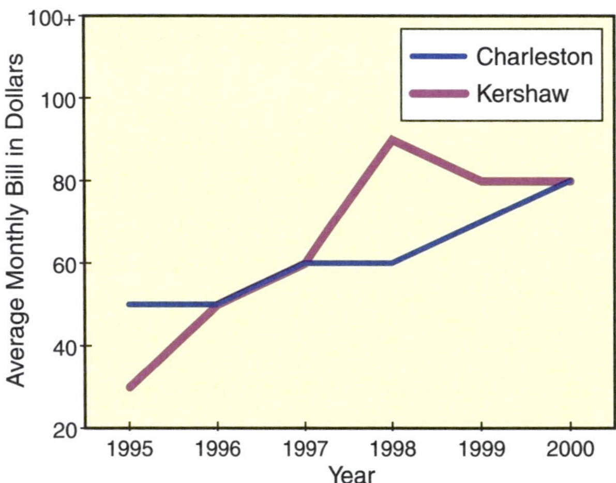

8. Between what two years did residents in Kershaw County see the greatest increase in their average monthly utility bills?

    (1) 1995 and 1996
    (2) 1996 and 1997
    (3) 1997 and 1998
    (4) 1998 and 1999
    (5) 1999 and 2000

9. What conclusion can you draw based on the information provided in the graph?

    (1) The cost of living is higher in Charleston County.
    (2) The cost of living is higher in Kershaw County.
    (3) Kershaw County was able to reduce its utility rates.
    (4) Charleston County utility rates did not cover the cost to provide electricity to everyone's home.
    (5) Kershaw County utility charges only dropped when people complained.

Tip

Look at the axes and diagonal lines to understand the relationship that is being illustrated. A line graph can depict upward, downward, or static trends. To interpret this information, locate the specific points on the graph and identify the trend that the graph represents.

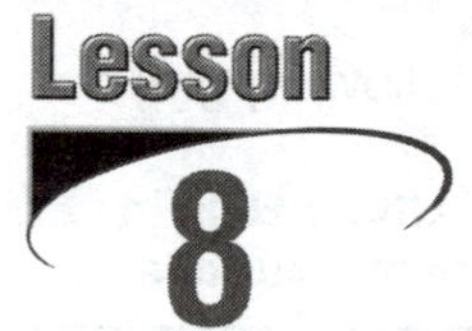

Lesson 8

Graphs
Line Graphs in Mathematics

A line graph is most useful in showing trends and development over a period of time. Line graphs can also show comparisons by including more than one trend line. For example, sales of two similar products in the same period of time can be compared on the same line graph by using two trend lines. Line graphs can depict different types of changes over time, such as stock market trends, population growth, job layoffs, or even how many hours people spend on the Internet.

Try this GED example. Choose the <u>one best answer</u> to each question. Then check your answers.

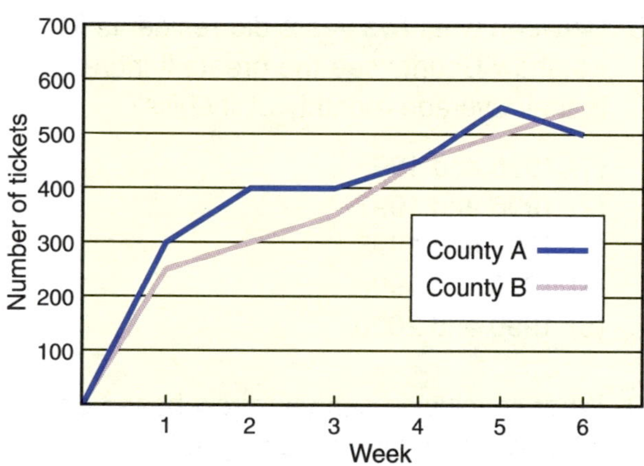

1. A new lottery was initiated in the state. Two counties charted their ticket sales for the first six weeks. From the data contained in the graph, between which two consecutive weeks was there the greatest increase in tickets sold in County A?

   Between

   (1) week 0 and 1
   (2) week 1 and 2
   (3) week 2 and 3
   (4) week 3 and 4
   (5) week 5 and 6

2. During which week was the same number of tickets sold in both counties?

   (1) week 1
   (2) week 2
   (3) week 3
   (4) week 4
   (5) week 5

3. Based on the trend lines in the graph, which of the following predictions can be made?

   (1) Ticket sales in County B will sharply decrease in week 7.
   (2) Ticket sales in County B will stay static in week 7.
   (3) Ticket sales in County B will increase in week 7.
   (4) Over 600 tickets will be sold in both County A and County B.
   (5) Fewer than 600 tickets will be sold in both County A and County B.

---

1. **(1)** The number of tickets increased by 300 from the inception of the lottery to the end of the first week. Options (2) and (4) show increases of fewer than 200 tickets. Option (3) shows no increase. Option (5) shows a decrease in ticket sales.

2. **(4)** Only for week 4 do both lines intersect, indicating that during that week sales in the two counties were equal. Options (1), (2), (3), and (5) depict different ticket sales amounts.

3. **(3)** Line graphs indicate trends. Because ticket sales in County B continue to increase, it is reasonable to predict a continued increase for week 7. Options (1), (2), (4), and (5) are not supported by the trend data.

Directions: Choose the <u>one best answer</u> to each question. <u>Questions 1 through 4</u> refer to the following graph.

Dividends for Stock G

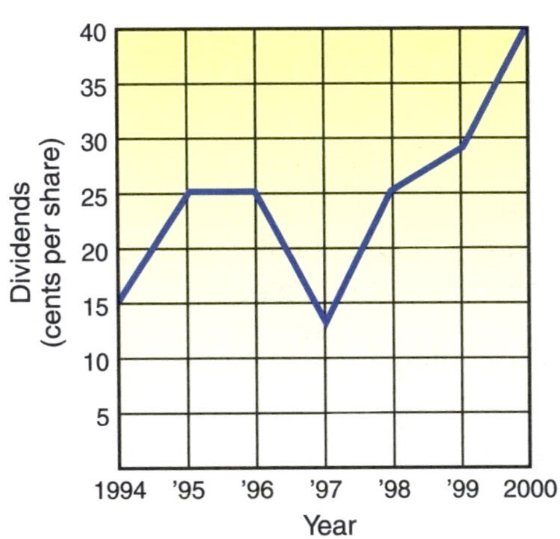

1. Between which two consecutive years did the amount of the dividend stay the same?

   Between

   (1) 1994 and 1995
   (2) 1995 and 1996
   (3) 1996 and 1997
   (4) 1998 and 1999
   (5) 1999 and 2000

2. What is the approximate difference in amount between the highest and lowest dividends paid?

   (1) 40
   (2) 25
   (3) 20
   (4) 5
   (5) 0

3. Between which two consecutive years did the amount of the dividend decrease?

   Between

   (1) 1994 and 1995
   (2) 1995 and 1996
   (3) 1996 and 1997
   (4) 1998 and 1999
   (5) 1999 and 2000

4. Based on the current trend depicted in the graph, which of the following would be the best prediction for dividends in 2002?

   (1) Dividends will show a major decrease.
   (2) Dividends will show a minimal decrease.
   (3) Dividends will stay static.
   (4) Dividends will show a major increase.
   (5) Dividends will show a minimal increase.

<u>Question 5</u> refers to the following graph.

Mathematics Test

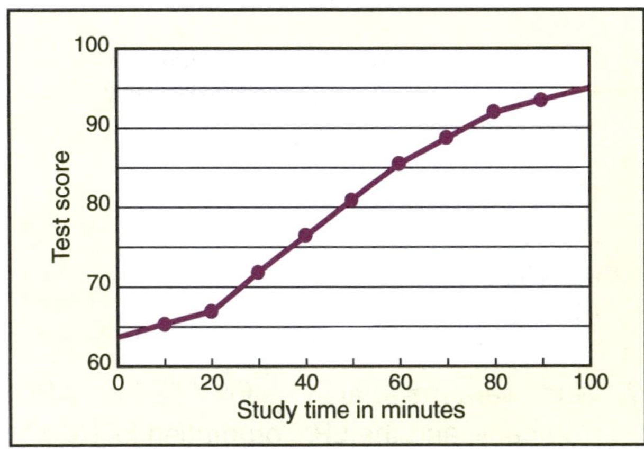

5. A survey was taken of the time students spent studying for a test in mathematics. Which statement best summarizes the data in the graph?

   (1) A positive relationship exists between study time and test scores.
   (2) A negative relationship exists between study time and test scores.
   (3) No relationship exists between study time and test scores.
   (4) Study time equals test scores.
   (5) Both positive and negative relationships exist between study times and test scores.

Company Sales

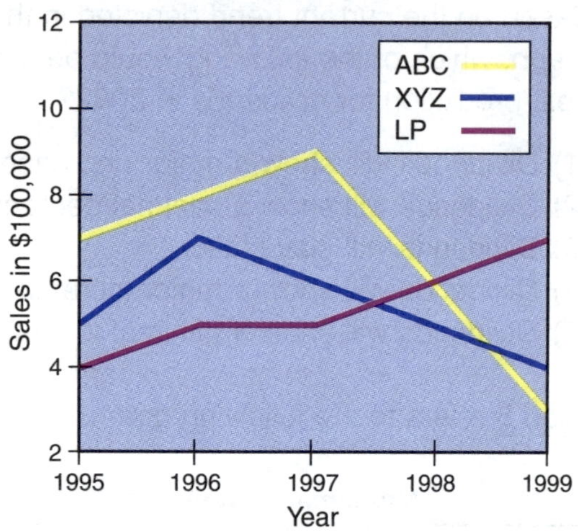

6. In what year were XYZ Inc. sales higher than the sales of the ABC Company?

    (1) 1995
    (2) 1996
    (3) 1997
    (4) 1998
    (5) 1999

7. What were the total sales for XYZ Inc., ABC Company, and the LP Corporation in 1998?

    Approximately

    (1)   17
    (2)   1,700
    (3)   17,000
    (4)   170,000
    (5)   1,700,000

8. For the periods shown on the graph, which of the following statements is true?

    (1) Only the ABC Company showed a steady increase in sales.
    (2) The ABC Company consistently exhibited the lowest sales.
    (3) The LP Corporation and XYZ Inc. had approximately the same total amount of sales.
    (4) The LP Corporation had lower total sales than XYZ Inc.
    (5) Only XYZ Inc. showed a decrease over the entire peroid.

9. What was the mean amount of sales for the ABC Company during the five years shown on the graph?

    Approximately

    (1) $ 500,000
    (2) $ 540,000
    (3) $ 660,000
    (4) $1,000,000
    (5) $2,700,000

10. If the trend for the LP Corporation continues as it did from 1997–1999, which of the following amounts best expresses the projection for 2000 sales?

    Approximately

    (1) $ 600,000
    (2) $ 700,000
    (3) $ 800,000
    (4) $ 900,000
    (5) $1,000,000

Tip

To predict trends for the future using a line graph, check to see if there is a regular pattern in the values on the graph. Connect the last few values on the graph and extend the line out to the point for which a prediction should be made. Then trace the corresponding value shown on the *y*-axis.

When drawing conclusions from graphs, remember to:
• Use only data located on the graph.
• Read the data correctly.
• Use correct units of measure.
• Determine correlations, not causes, since graphs do not depict causes.
• Report facts rather than reasons since graphs do not show why things occur.

Graphs
Circle Graphs in Social Studies and Science

If you look through textbooks for courses such as chemistry, biology, physical science, history, and economics, you will see a variety of tables, graphs, and charts. One common type of graph is the circle graph, also called a pie chart. Circle graphs are used to represent a part-to-whole relationship. Circle graphs show at a glance the relative sizes of different categories and how these parts are combined to make a whole.

When reading a circle graph, look for the following pieces of information: the graph title, individual sectors and their relative sizes, and the sector labels. Remember, since circle graphs show percentages, the whole graph equals 100% of the topic and each sector is a lesser percentage.

Try these sample GED items. Choose the <u>one best answer</u> to each question. Then check your answers.

Part of the study of genetics involves being able to predict the appearance (phenotype) and genetics (genotype) of the offspring of animals or people. Currently, the study of genetics has identified three known genes for eye color: the green/blue eye color gene, the brown eye color gene, and the brown/blue eye color gene. A second gene for green has also been proposed; however, genes for gray and hazel eye colors have not yet been explained.

Eye Color

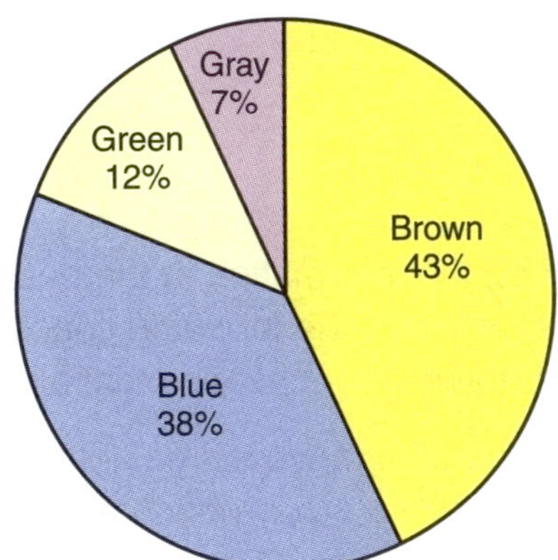

1. In this graph showing the results of a study of eye color in 15,000 people, which eye color was dominant?

   (1) blue
   (2) brown
   (3) green
   (4) gray
   (5) None of the colors was dominant.

2. Which of the following statements is supported by the information provided in the passage and graph?

   (1) Four different genes for eye color have been identified.
   (2) Genes do not exist for the eye colors of gray and hazel.
   (3) Phenotype is more important in the study of genetics than genotype.
   (4) There are many different phenotypes of eye color.
   (5) All of the different genes for eye color have been identified.

---

1. **(2)** The number of individuals in the survey with brown eyes was greater than any of the other eye colors reported. Options (1), (3), and (4) are smaller percentages than option (2). Option (5) contradicts information in the graph.

2. **(4)** Phenotype refers to the appearance of a trait. Many eye colors do not currently have identified genes. The passage refutes options (1), (2), and (5). Option (3) is incorrect because the passage does not state that one part of genetics is more important than another.

Directions: Choose the <u>one best answer</u> to each question. Questions 1 through 4 refer to the following passage and graph.

The Election of 1824

Election results have often been controversial. One such election was the presidential election of 1824. Four candidates were on the ballot—Andrew Jackson, Henry Clay, John Quincy Adams, and William Crawford. Andrew Jackson won the most popular votes but failed to win a majority and did not have enough electoral votes to win. Clay urged his supporters to cast their electoral votes for Adams, who was elected president. An important outcome of the election was that Jackson and his supporters joined together to form the Democratic Party and campaigned among workers and farmers who had not previously voted. This effort with the "common" man helped Jackson defeat Adams in 1828 to win the presidential election.

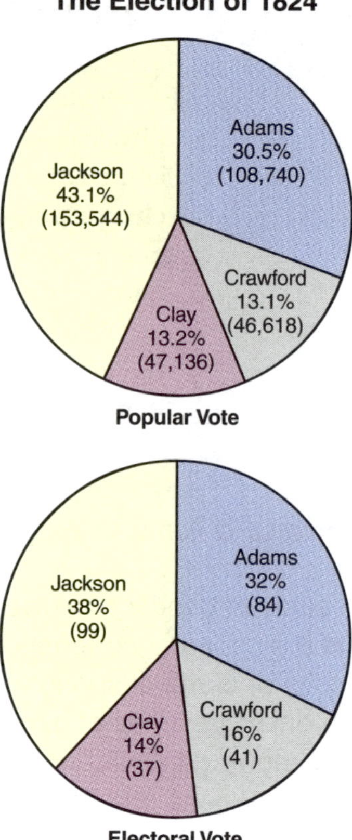

The Election of 1824

1. Which of the following statements is most relevant to the outcome of the 1824 election?

   (1) No candidate won at least 50% of the popular vote.
   (2) Two hundred and sixty-one electoral votes were cast in the 1824 election.
   (3) All of the candidates were part of the same political party.
   (4) Both popular and electoral votes have always been used in election results.
   (5) Four candidates were contenders for the 1824 presidential election.

2. How many electoral votes did Adams receive from Clay?

   (1) 47,136
   (2) 46,618
   (3)   41
   (4)   37
   (5)   14

3. How many total electoral votes were possible in the 1824 election?

   (1) 356,040
   (2)   261
   (3)   121
   (4)   99
   (5)   84

4. Based on the information in the passage and graphs, which of the following conclusions can be drawn about presidential elections?

   (1) The candidate with a majority of the popular vote always becomes president.
   (2) The percentage of popular vote determines the percentage of electoral votes received.
   (3) The electoral college makes the final decision on presidential elections.
   (4) Plurality of the popular vote is more important than majority of popular vote.
   (5) Presidential elections are never won by the individual with the majority of the popular vote.

Earth's Elements

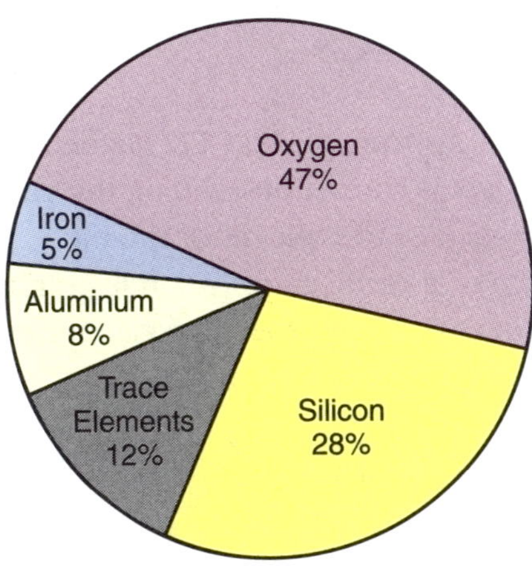

5. Earth's crust contains many different elements. Which of the following is most abundant?

   (1) iron, aluminum, and trace elements
   (2) silicon and trace elements
   (3) trace elements
   (4) oxygen
   (5) silicon

6. Which of the following elements compose one fourth of the elements contained in Earth's crust?

   (1) iron, aluminum, and trace elements
   (2) aluminum and trace elements
   (3) trace elements and silicon
   (4) oxygen
   (5) silicon, trace elements, and aluminum

Questions 7 and 8 refer to the following passage and graph.

Each year an estimated 79 million people in the U.S. become ill from food-related diseases due to food contaminated by microbes. About 14.3 million of the cases are tied to food-borne bacteria, parasites, and viruses. While foods are generally safe if handled and stored properly, they are not sterile. Poor hygiene contributes to many food-related outbreaks as does the improper cooking and care of food.

Causes of Food-Related Diseases

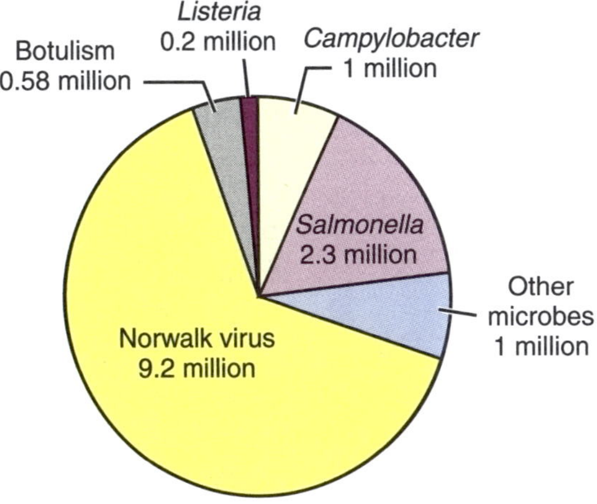

7. Based on the above information, which of the following is an effective method of preventing microbial contamination during food production?

   (1) pasteurization and irradiation
   (2) poor hygiene
   (3) not serving shellfish
   (4) identifying the other microbes
   (5) purchasing foods from commercial vendors

8. What causes over half of the food-related diseases?

   (1) *Campylobacter* and *Salmonella*
   (2) botulism and *Salmonella*
   (3) *Listeria, Campylobacter,* and other microbes
   (4) Norwalk virus
   (5) *Salmonella*

Tip

In studying circle graphs, ask the following questions:
• What does the entire circle represent?
• What do the various parts, or sectors, of the circle represent?
• How do the percentages of each of the sectors compare?

Lesson 10

Graphs
Circle Graphs in Mathematics

Circle graphs, also known as pie charts, appear on the GED Mathematics test. In a circle graph, the circle equals 100%. Data is shown by dividing the circle into sectors and placing one type of data into each of the "pieces of the pie."

Budgets are often depicted in the form of a circle graph. A circle graph quickly shows how much money is being spent in each of the specified categories. By showing how the different sectors, or "slices of the pie," compare to one another, a circle graph can reveal priorities.

Questions on the GED test will ask you to answer questions based on circle graphs.

Try this GED example. Choose the <u>one best answer</u> to each question. Then check your answers.

Club Members

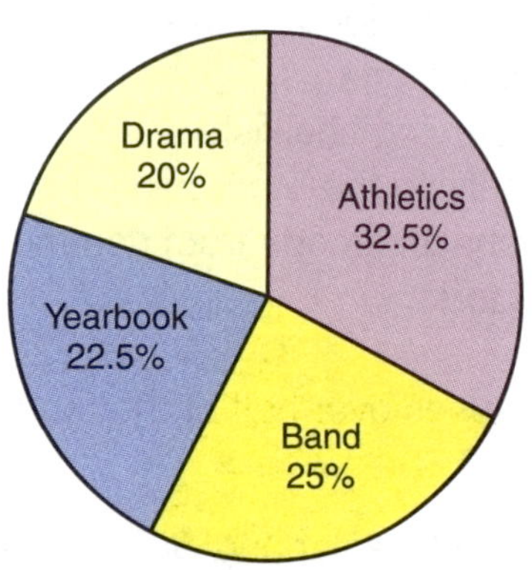

A high school has 1,000 students. Six hundred students are involved in four of the school's clubs or organizations.

1. How many students are involved in athletics and band?

   (1)   58
   (2) 150
   (3) 195
   (4) 345
   (5) 575

2. What percentage of the total student body belongs to the drama club?

   (1)   0.08%
   (2)   0.8%
   (3) 12%
   (4)   0.20%
   (5) 20%

---

1. (4) Add the percentage of students in athletics and band (57.5%) and then multiply the total number of students involved in organizations (600) by the percentage (57.5%). Options (1), (2), and (3) use an incorrect formula. Option (5) uses the entire student body as a base rather than the number of students currently in activities.

2. (3) The graph shows membership in the drama club is 20% of the students inolved in clubs:

$$600 \times 20\% = 120 \text{ students}$$

The total student body is 1,000.

$$\frac{120}{1,000} = \frac{x}{100\%}$$
$$x = 12\%$$

GED Skill Book • Interpreting Visual Information

Circle Graphs in Mathematics

Directions: Choose the <u>one best answer</u> to each question. Questions 1 through 5 refer to the following graph.

Annual Budget for Manufacturing Firm
(Total Budget 6.3 million dollars)

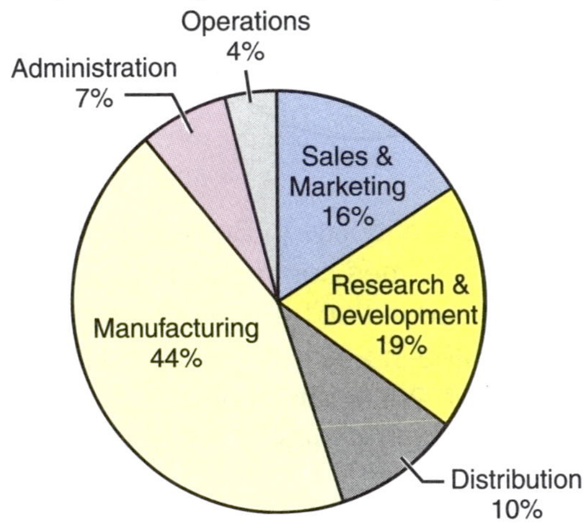

1. Which of the above represents the largest share of expenses?

    (1) Sales & Marketing
    (2) Research & Development
    (3) Sales & Marketing and Research & Development
    (4) Distribution, Administration, and Operations
    (5) Manufacturing

2. Which category receives approximately 1.2 million dollars of the budget?

    (1) Sales & Marketing
    (2) Research & Development
    (3) Distribution
    (4) Manufacturing
    (5) Administration and Operations

3. Which two categories together represent about 50% of all spending?

    (1) Sales & Marketing and Research & Development
    (2) Sales & Marketing, Research & Development, and Distribution
    (3) Manufacturing and Distribution
    (4) Manufacturing and Administration
    (5) Manufacturing and Sales & Marketing

4. A new product needs to be manufactured for a customer, which will require an increase in the Manufacturing budget. If the Manufacturing budget is increased to 52.5% of the total budget, what dollar amount will need to be deducted from the budget's other categories?

    (1) $ 8.50
    (2) $ 53.55
    (3) $ 535.50
    (4) $ 53,550.00
    (5) $535,500.00

5. For the upcoming year, the manufacturing firm plans to increase their total budget by $700,000. If the division of funding remains the same for each category, what will be the budget for Administration and Operations?

    (1) $770,000
    (2) $693,000
    (3) $490,000
    (4) $ 77,000
    (5) $ 69,300

Circle graphs are a simple but effective way of displaying percentages.

Crime Statistics for 2000 and 2001

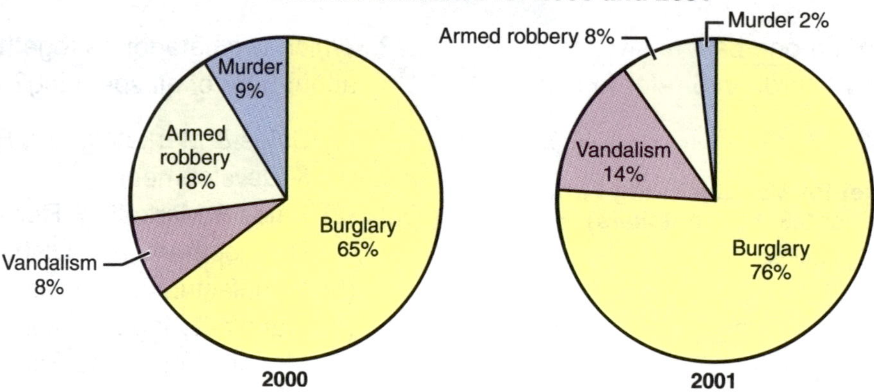

6. The graphs show crime statistics for the town of Beale. In 2000, a total of 100 crimes were committed in Beale. How many of them were burglary?

   (1)   0.65
   (2)   6.5
   (3)   65
   (4)   91
   (5) 100

7. The chief of police in Beale compared the types of crimes committed in 2000 to those committed in 2001. Eighty crimes were committed in 2001 as compared to 100 crimes in 2000. Which type of crime showed the greatest decrease in number?

   (1) armed robbery
   (2) burglary
   (3) murder
   (4) vandalism
   (5) None showed a decrease in number.

Questions 8 and 9 refer to the following graph.

Survey Results for After-School Daycare

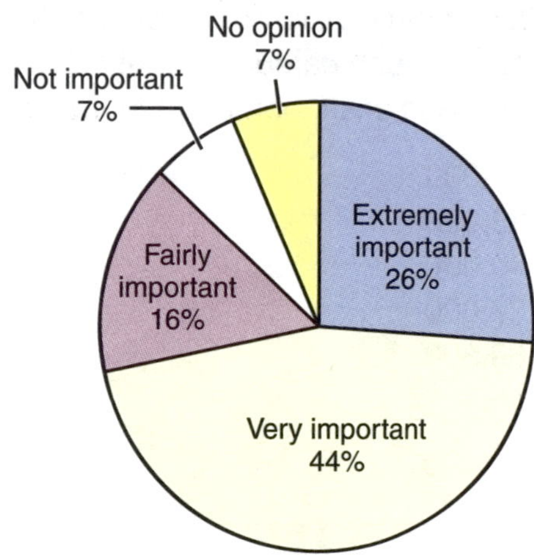

8. Which of the categories had the greatest frequency?

   (1) Extremely important
   (2) Very important
   (3) Fairly important
   (4) Not important
   (5) No opinion

9. Two hundred adults responded to a survey about the importance of after-school daycare at their child's school. What percent of parents felt that after-school daycare had at least some importance?

   (1) less than 50%
   (2) approximately 50%
   (3) exactly 66%
   (4) less than 75%
   (5) more than 75%

Tip

Remember that circle graphs require an understanding of how the parts of the graph make up a whole. All of the information must be accounted for by the circle graph since the entire graph represents 100%.

Graphs
Pictographs in Social Studies, Science, and Mathematics

A pictograph is a special kind of graph that displays information using pictures or symbols. Pictographs are used to compare and contrast information as well as to show trends or changes in data. When interpreting data on a pictograph, read the title to get the main idea of the pictograph and review the key or legend to understand what the symbols or pictures represent. Pictographs will often use a portion of a symbol to represent a fraction of the total unit. For example, if one book symbol equals 10 books read, one-half of a symbol would represent 5 books read.

The GED test will ask you to answer questions based on pictographs.

Try this GED example. Choose the <u>one best answer</u> to each question. Then check your answers.

To raise money for new playground equipment, the parents at Zena Elementary School sold four types of snacks: popcorn, cookies, pretzels, and potato chips. Each snack sold for $1.00.

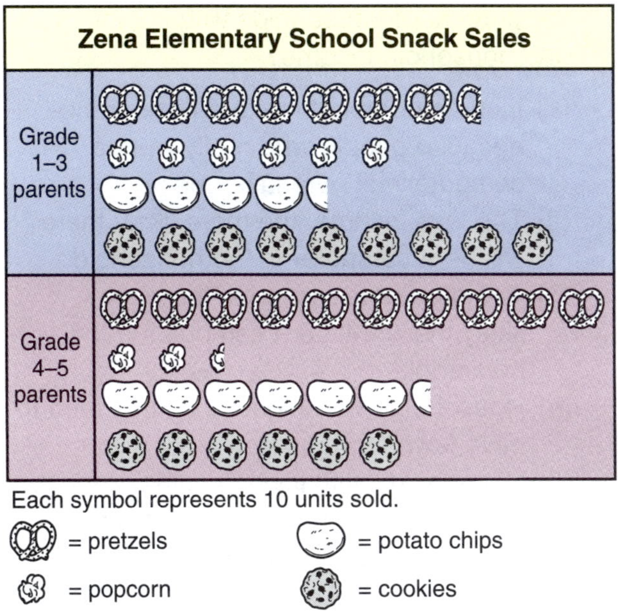

Zena Elementary School Snack Sales

Grade 1–3 parents

Grade 4–5 parents

Each symbol represents 10 units sold.

= pretzels   = potato chips

= popcorn   = cookies

1. From the data contained in the graph, which two products generated the greatest sales?

   (1) pretzels and cookies
   (2) popcorn and cookies
   (3) cookies and potato chips
   (4) pretzels and potato chips
   (5) popcorn and potato chips

2. Approximately what percent of total sales came from the sale of pretzels?

   (1) 20%
   (2) 25%
   (3) 34%
   (4) 40%
   (5) 50%

---

1. **(1)** 325 units of pretzels and cookies were sold. Total sales for option (2) was 235; option (3) was 260; option (4) was 285; and option (5) was 195.

2. **(3)** 520 total units of snacks were sold. 175 units of pretzels were sold. This amount is approximately 34% of 520. Options (1), (2), (4), and (5) use incorrect calculations.

Pictographs in Social Studies, Science, and Mathematics

Directions: Choose the <u>one best answer</u> to each question. <u>Questions 1 and 2</u> refer to the following graph.

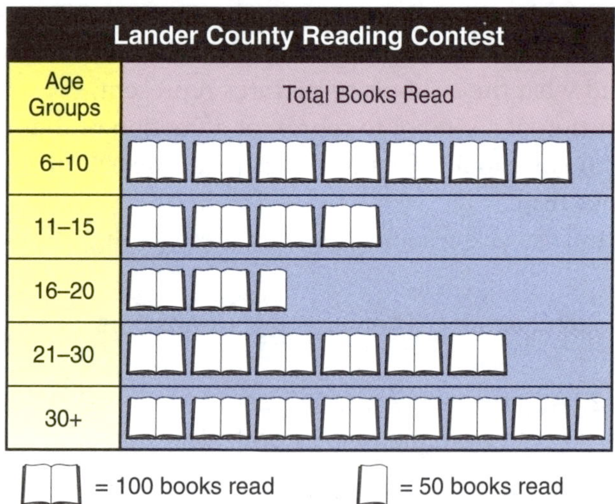

1. Lander County conducted a reading contest. Based on the information in the graph, which of the following age groups read the most books?

   (1) 6–10
   (2) 11–15
   (3) 16–20
   (4) 21–30
   (5) 30+

2. Based on the data in the graph, which statement most accurately reflects the reading habits of residents in Lander County?

   (1) The most avid readers are children between the ages of 6 and 10.
   (2) Children ages 11 to 15 on average read as many books as younger children.
   (3) Younger children and adults over 30 represent the individuals who read the most books.
   (4) As people grow older, they read less.
   (5) Reading habits are not affected by age.

Questions 3 and 4 refer to the following graph.

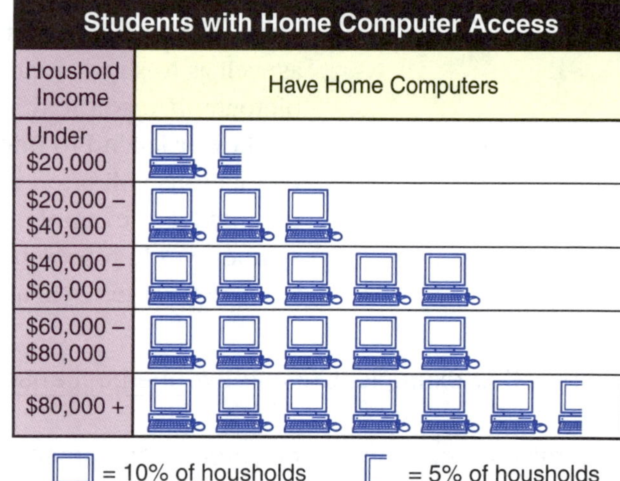

3. Based on the graph, which statement most accurately reflects the relationship between the percent of households with computers and household income?

   (1) Income does not make any difference because people who really want a computer will purchase one.
   (2) The less income, the more likely there will be a computer in the household.
   (3) The greater the income, the more likely there will be a computer in the household.
   (4) Households with higher incomes tend to have fewer computers.
   (5) Households with lower incomes tend to purchase computers as frequently as higher-income households.

4. Which household income group has the greatest percentage of home computers?

   (1) less than $20,000
   (2) $20,000–$40,000
   (3) $40,000–$60,000
   (4) $60,000–$80,000
   (5) $80,000+

Questions 5 through 7 refer to the following graph.

Snow Fall
Week 1 — ❄❄❄❄❄
Week 2 — ❄❄❄
Week 3 — ❄
Week 4 — ❄❄❄❄❄❄❄❄❄❄ ❄❄
Week 5 — ❄❄❄❄❄❄❄❄❄❄
Week 6 — ❄❄❄❄❄❄❄❄❄❄ ❄❄❄❄

❄ = 1 inch of snow

5. This graph shows a period of six weeks beginning the second week of January. When did the most snow fall?

   (1) Week 1
   (2) Week 2
   (3) Week 4
   (4) Week 5
   (5) Week 6

6. What was the mean weekly snowfall during the six-week period?

   (1) 40 inches
   (2) 20 inches
   (3) 10.5 inches
   (4) 7 inches
   (5) 6 inches

7. Which of the following statements most accurately reflects the weather pattern during the six-week period?

   (1) The weather stayed the same throughout the six-week period.
   (2) The weather changed drastically from week to week.
   (3) The amount of snow steadily decreased during the six-week period.
   (4) The amount of snow increased significantly after week three.
   (5) The amount of snow decreased after week three.

Questions 8 and 9 refer to the following graph.

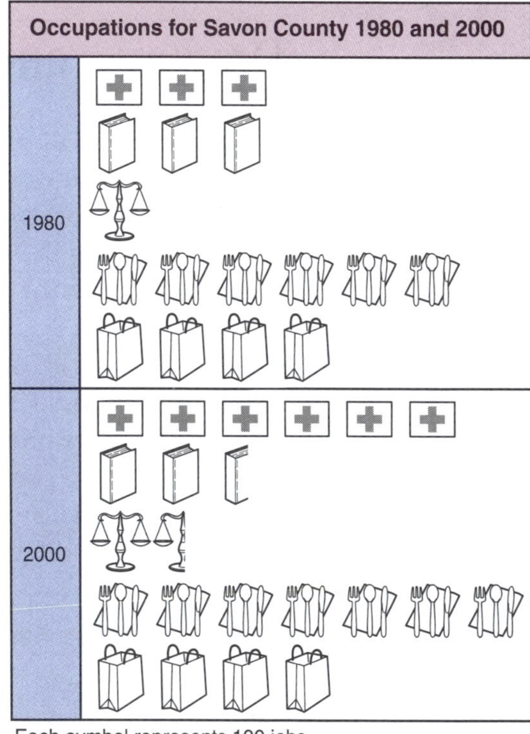

Each symbol represents 100 jobs.

8. Which occupation experienced the greatest decrease in total number of jobs?

   (1) healthcare
   (2) teaching
   (3) legal profession
   (4) restaurant and service industry
   (5) retail sales

9. Which occupation experienced the greatest percentage of growth?

   (1) healthcare
   (2) teaching
   (3) legal profession
   (4) restaurant and service industry
   (5) retail sales

Drawings and Diagrams
Drawings and Diagrams in Social Studies

Drawings and diagrams are two examples of visual representations that provide a pictorial view of a subject. Drawings and diagrams often provide very specific details. For example, think of the directions you receive for assembling a bicycle. Following the written directions may prove difficult, but a drawing or diagram can make the assembly process much easier.

Drawings and diagrams provide more details than might be provided in a passage. A flowchart is a specific type of diagram that is often used to show the steps in a process, such as how a bill becomes a law. Another type of diagram is a timeline. Timelines provide a short synopsis of events over a specified period of time.

The GED Social Studies test will ask you to answer questions based on different types of drawings and diagrams.

Try this GED example. Choose the <u>one best answer</u> to the question. Then check your answer.

Trade Balance

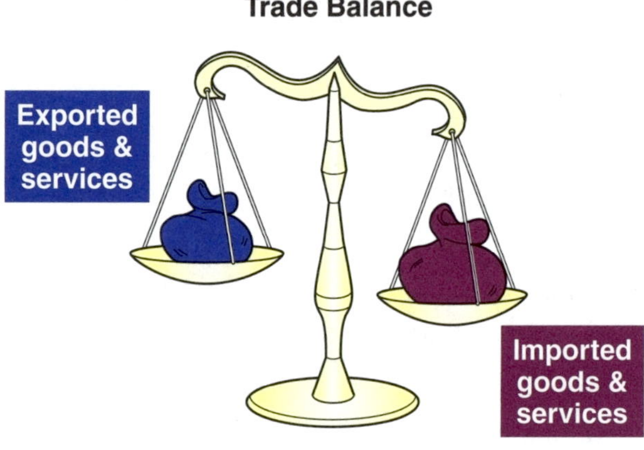

The importing and exporting of goods and services is an essential part of the U.S. economy. Each year the United States exports billions of dollars worth of goods and services. It also imports billions of dollars worth of goods and services. Goods and services sent to other countries create revenue and jobs for Americans. Likewise, Americans often want goods and services that are created elsewhere, so these goods and services must be imported. A trade deficit occurs when there is an imbalance between exports and imports.

1. Based on the drawing, what would the United States need to do to show a balance of trade with other countries?

   (1) purchase more services from other countries
   (2) produce more goods for sale in the United States
   (3) provide more services to Americans living in foreign countries
   (4) reduce export of goods and services to other countries
   (5) increase the amount of goods and services exported to other countries

---

1. (5) The scales in the drawing are tipped in favor of imported goods and services. To correct the imbalance, the United States would need to increase exports. Options (1) and (4) would further increase the trade imbalance. Options (2) and (3) are not factors in trade with other countries.

Drawings and Diagrams in Social Studies

<u>Directions</u>: Choose the <u>one best answer</u> to each question. <u>Questions 1 and 2</u> refer to the following timeline.

Struggle Toward Suffrage

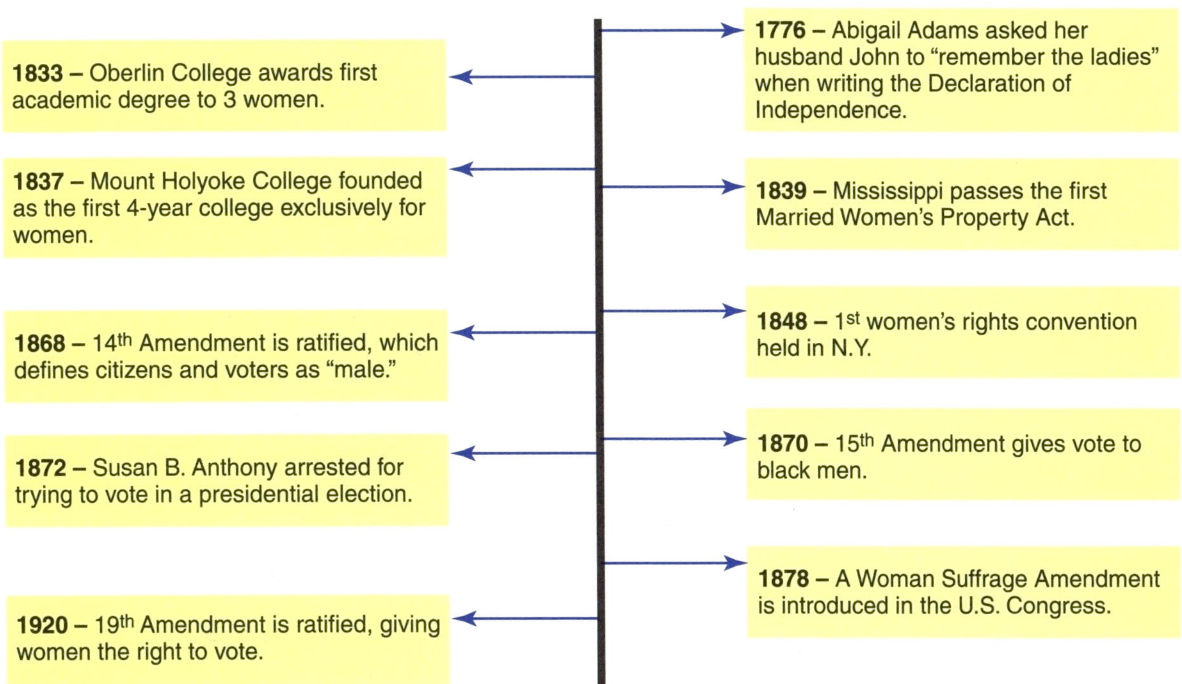

1. Which of the following statements is supported by the information in the timeline?

   (1) Institutions of higher learning for women were established years before women gained the right to vote.
   (2) It was more difficult for black men to earn the right to vote than for women.
   (3) The Woman Suffrage Amendment would have been ratified earlier if more women had supported it.
   (4) In the 1800s, women were only allowed to enroll in colleges that were exclusively designed for women.
   (5) The 14th Amendment was repealed to make way for the 19th Amendment.

2. After the Civil War, many women's rights leaders were upset because of their continuing failure to gain the right to vote despite the gains made by other segments of the population. Which of the following events created extreme disappointment because of how women had worked to eliminate slavery?

   (1) the ratification of the 14th Amendment which defined citizens and voters as "males"
   (2) the arrest of Susan B. Anthony
   (3) the ratification of the 15th Amendment, which gave the right to vote to black men
   (4) the failure of John Adams to include women in the Declaration of Independence
   (5) the passage of the first Married Women's Property Act

Tip

Timelines can display events in a horizontal or vertical format.

Questions 3 and 4 refer to the following flowchart and passage.

How a Bill Becomes Law

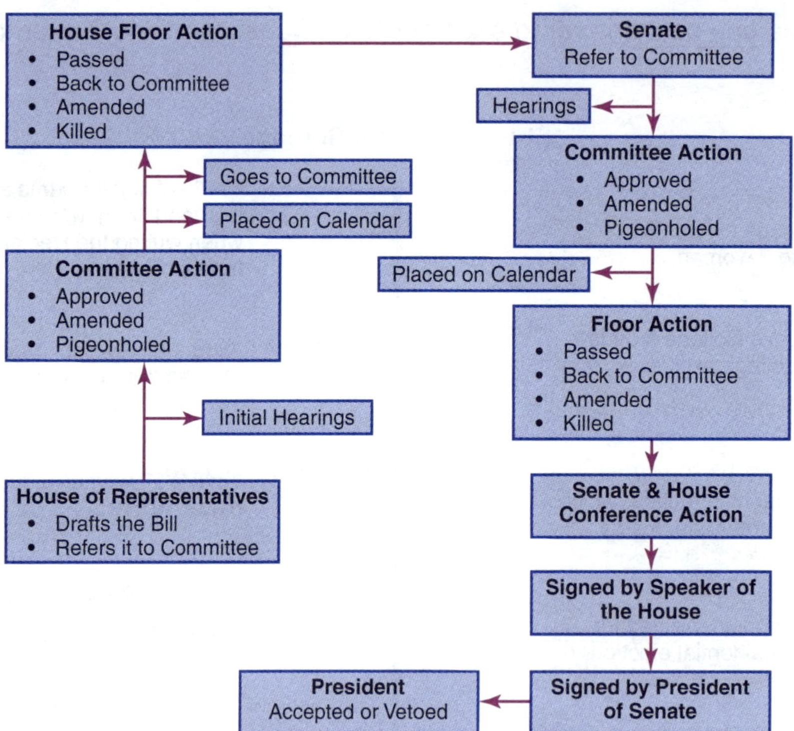

Anyone may draft a bill, but only members of Congress can introduce legislation. Bills may be introduced in either the House or the Senate. The legislative process is very cumbersome. However, if a bill can make it through initial committee action, it has a greater likelihood of making it through the entire process. As a result, it may take months or even years for a bill to make its way through the entire process and be signed into law by the president of the United States. Throughout the process, there are opportunities for the House and Senate to agree and disagree about specific parts of the bill.

3. According to the flowchart, there are many points in the process where a bill may be stopped. At what point is a bill most likely to receive its greatest scrutiny?

(1) during committee action
(2) during floor action
(3) during the conference committee between the House and Senate
(4) when the president decides to approve or veto
(5) when the bill comes up for debate

4. Which of the following conclusions is supported by the information in the flowchart and passage?

(1) A bill may only be drafted by a committee in the House of Representatives.
(2) A bill may be submitted by the president if the House and Senate agree.
(3) A bill does not have to go through the entire legislative process if it is approved in the initial hearings.
(4) The legislative process is complicated and can take a long time to complete.
(5) The legislative process should be changed to reflect current needs of the U.S.

Tip

Always read the captions and labels on drawings and diagrams. Both captions and labels may provide details needed to answer questions. Labels can help you understand the parts of the diagram or the steps included in a drawing.

Drawings and Diagrams
Drawings and Diagrams in Science

Scientific drawings and flowcharts provide a visual representation of information. Flowcharts and process diagrams enable the reader to see how something works or the steps that must be taken in a process. Both flowcharts and process diagrams provide descriptions in picture format.

Often flowcharts or process diagrams are accompanied by text that enables the writer to provide more detail about the topic. The GED Science test uses scientific drawings and process diagrams to expand on information provided in a passage or text. They are also used to provide a step-by-step process for something. If the text is difficult to read, study the diagram or flowchart to help you understand the information.

The GED test will ask you to answer questions based on drawings, diagrams, and flowcharts.

Try this GED example. Choose the one best answer to the question. Then check your answer.

Birth of a Hurricane

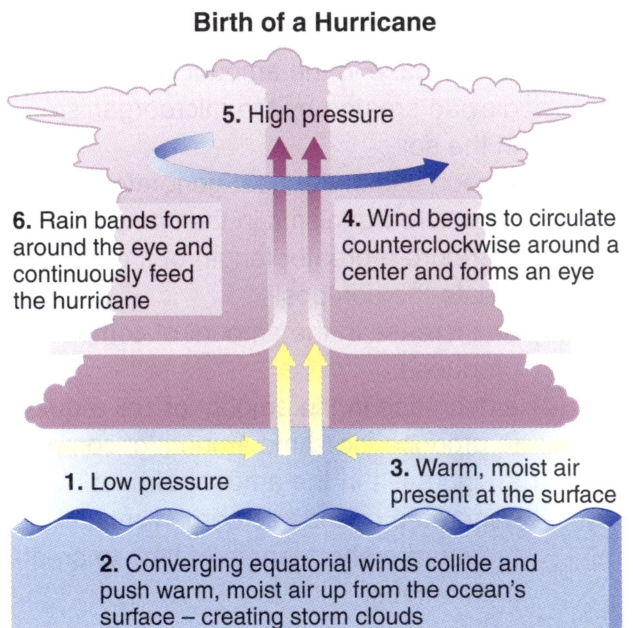

1. Based on the diagram, what three events must occur for a hurricane to form?

(1) warm, humid ocean air, converging winds, and similar pressure at the surface and upper atmosphere

(2) low pressure at the surface, high pressure in the upper atmosphere, and rain bands to feed the hurricane

(3) converging equatorial winds, low pressure at the surface, and wind circulation to form an eye

(4) warm, humid ocean air, converging winds, and differences in pressure at the surface and the upper atmosphere

(5) surface temperature above 80°, warm, moist air creating storm clouds, and circulating winds that form an eye

A hurricane is a powerful storm with swirling winds that forms over warm ocean water. These storms are called hurricanes when they occur over the North Atlantic Ocean, the Caribbean Sea, the Gulf of Mexico, and the northeastern Pacific Ocean. The same kind of storms are known as typhoons if they occur in the northwestern Pacific Ocean and as tropical cyclones if they occur near Australia or in the Indian Ocean.

1. (3) Look at the diagram. Steps 5 and 6 are the result of the formation of the hurricane, not part of its beginning. Option (1) indicates that the pressure between the upper and lower atmosphere is the same, which is not supported by the diagram. Options (2) and (4) include elements that are a result of a hurricane's formation. Option (5) includes data not found in the diagram.

Directions: Choose the <u>one best answer</u> to each question. <u>Questions 1 and 2</u> refer to the following diagram and passage.

The Composting Process

Composting is one way that anyone can recycle waste material, reduce the amount of solid waste sent to landfills, and produce rich, organic material that can be used to enhance soil. There are four essential elements for creating compost: organic waste, water, air (oxygen), and soil that contains microorganisms. These four elements combine to create the perfect environment for the natural process of decay to occur.

During composting, microorganisms such as bacteria and fungi from soil consume the organic waste and break it down into smaller particles. These microorganisms require water and air to live and multiply. As they break down the organic waste, the bacteria and fungi give off carbon dioxide and heat that helps speed up the process of decay, transforming everyday waste into rich compost.

1. Based on the information in the diagram and passage, which of the following generates the heat required for composting to occur?

   (1) kitchen waste, such as fruits and vegetables
   (2) warm water
   (3) high temperatures in the summer time
   (4) microorganisms in the soil using oxygen and water to create carbon dioxide
   (5) newspapers, leaves, and grass

2. More oxygen is introduced into the compost bin whenever the material is "stirred" or turned using a shovel or rake. Likewise, the less the compost is turned, the less oxygen is introduced to the compost. Which of the following would most likely result from a decreased level of oxygen in a compost bin?

   (1) an increase in the amount of carbon dioxide created by the microorganisms in the soil
   (2) a decrease in the heat generated by the microorganisms in the compost, therefore a greater length of time to create the compost
   (3) an increase in the amount of compost produced
   (4) a decrease in the amount of soil required to produce the same amount of compost
   (5) an increase in the amount of heat generated by the microorganisms, therefore a short length of time to create the compost

Tip

Flowcharts and other process diagrams include directional arrows to show the order or sequence in which events in the process occur. Pay close attention to directional arrows.

Questions 3 and 4 refer to the following text and diagram.

The USDA Food Pyramid is a guide for making good food choices. The Food Pyramid provides general guidelines about the different types and quantities of food people should eat every day for the healthiest diet possible.

In addition to fats, such as oil or butter, meats and diary products are generally higher in fat than fruits or vegetables. However, vegetables are sometimes cooked in oil, which increases their level of fat. It is important that people pay attention to the foods they choose to eat and how those foods are prepared in order to make the smartest food choices for a healthy diet. The Food Pyramid shows how to focus on healthier food choices.

The USDA Food Pyramid

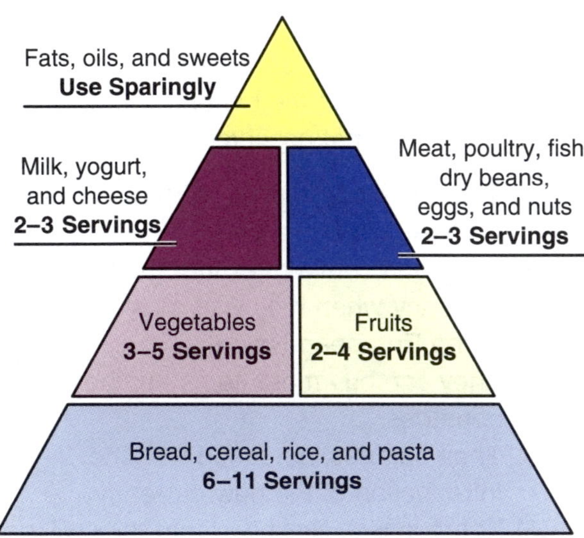

3. Based on the diagram, which of the following food combinations would be the healthiest choice for lunch?

   (1) pasta with meat sauce and cheese
   (2) grilled chicken with steamed vegetables
   (3) tuna salad on white bread with chips
   (4) hamburger and French-fries
   (5) diet soda and candy bar

4. Carol has been on a diet for 2 months. In that time, she has managed to lose 6 pounds. Carol's daily diet consists of the following:

   6 servings of bread, cereal, rice, or pasta
   4 servings of vegetables
   2 servings of fruit
   2 servings of milk or cheese
   4 servings of meat, poultry, fish
   2 servings of fats, oils and sweets

Which of the following would be the most effective changes in Carol's diet if she wants to lose more weight?

She should

   (1) increase the servings of vegetables and fruit to increase the amount of natural sugar in her diet and increase her metabolism
   (2) increase the servings of vegetables and reduce the servings of bread and cereal to give her more complex carbohydrates and more energy
   (3) increase the servings of fruit and milk or cheese to increase her protein level
   (4) decrease the servings of meat, poultry, and fish and the servings of fats, oils, and sweets to more closely align with the guidelines
   (5) increase the servings of all food groups so that her metabolism will increase

Before answering any GED questions based on drawings or diagrams, review the drawing or diagram. Make sure you read all titles, captions, and written descriptions. See if you can describe in your own words the information or process the drawing or diagram displays. Once you can summarize the drawing or diagram, you will better be able to answer.

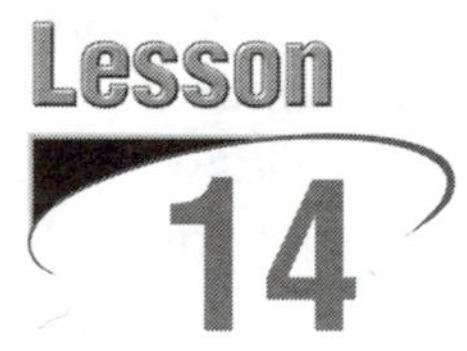

Maps
Maps in Social Studies

Maps are tools that can serve a variety of functions. For example, road maps help us find the easiest route from one location to another; political maps show the boundaries between counties, states, or countries; and topographic maps show the elevation of an area.

In social studies, maps are a visual way to provide detailed and complex information about many things, such as: geographic location, land use, natural resources, agricultural products, manufacturing areas, population, and climate. Maps may also be used to show specialized information about historical and political events: for example, the countries that belong to the North Atlantic Treaty Organization (NATO), the empire of Alexander the Great, or the route of the Lewis and Clark expedition.

The GED Social Studies test will ask you to answer questions based on maps.

Try this GED example. Choose the one best answer to the question. Then check your answer.

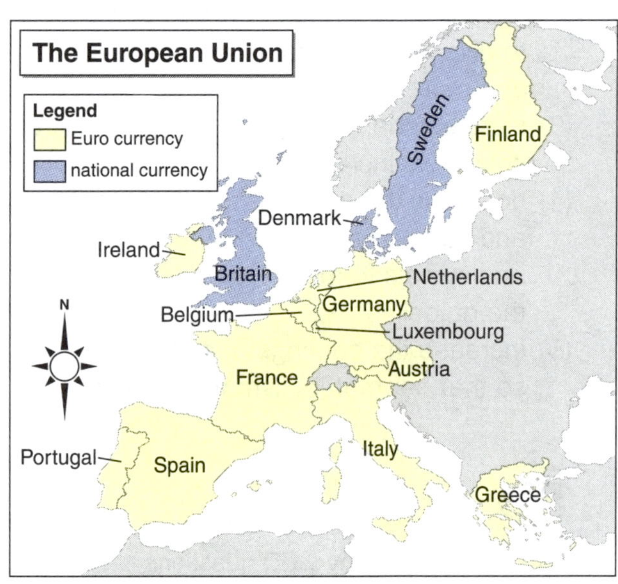

1. Based on the information in the map and passage, what are the benefits to the citizens of the nations that accepted the Euro?

   (1) Their new currency is worth more now than the old currency.
   (2) They don't have to exchange their currency when they visit other countries in the European Union.
   (3) They can buy more items in other countries.
   (4) Their salaries increased with the introduction of the new currency.
   (5) There is less likelihood that they will get counterfeit currency.

In February 1992, the Treaty of European Union was signed. Fifteen European nations joined together to produce a timetable that would lead to economic and monetary unity in Europe. On January 1, 2002, twelve European Union member nations introduced Euro notes and coins. Britain, Sweden, and Denmark retained their own national currencies. Within days of the launch of the Euro notes and coins, more than 75% of all commercial transactions in the twelve nations used Euros, putting to rest many of the concerns about the acceptance of the single currency.

1. (2) Before 2002, the citizens of the twelve nations had twelve different currencies. When travelers went from one country to another, they often had to exchange currency to buy goods or services. With a single currency, consumers can use the same coins and notes in every country. The passage does not address the worth of the new currency (options 1 and 3) nor its effect on counterfeiting (option 5). Establishing a new currency has no automatic effect on citizens' salaries (option 4).

Directions: Choose the <u>one best answer</u> to each question. <u>Questions 1 and 2</u> refer to the following map and passage.

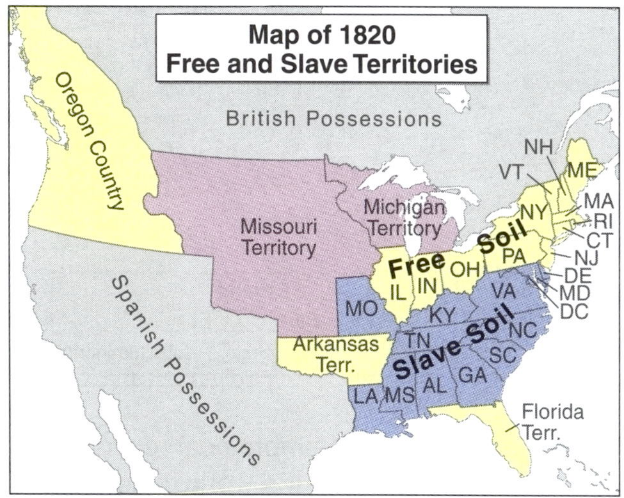

In the 1800s, the United States was experiencing serious problems, at the heart of which was the issue of slavery. As new territories opened up, the question arose as to whether or not new territories should permit slavery. Congress worked hard to find ways to keep the nation together. In 1820, the Missouri Compromise was passed allowing Missouri to enter as a slave state and Maine as a free state, thus balancing power between those supporting and opposing slavery. However, in subsequent legislation, a provision was put in place to prohibit slavery in the rest of the Louisiana Purchase north of Missouri.

Congress later passed the Compromise of 1850 which admitted one more free and one more slave state. It also abolished the slave trade in the District of Columbia, but did not decide whether slavery was constitutional. The Compromise of 1850 also included the Fugitive Slave Act which required citizens to help recover fugitive slaves. The Fugitive Slave Act pushed more people to oppose slavery. The Compromise of 1850 temporarily kept the nation together, but it further divided anti- and pro-slavery forces. Eventually this rift led to the Civil War.

1. Based on the map and passage, what was one of the greatest factors in turning people against slavery?

   (1) the opening of more free states than slave states
   (2) the Ordinance of 1787 that made the Michigan Territory free of slavery
   (3) the abolition of slave trade in the District of Columbia
   (4) the passage of the Fugitive Slave Act that required all citizens to return fugitive slaves to their owners
   (5) the opening of Spanish Possessions to slavery

2. What was one of the greatest concerns about whether or not to allow slavery in new territories?

   (1) slave states would produce more goods and free states would have to purchase those goods
   (2) an imbalance of power would result between free and slave states and their representatives in Congress
   (3) all slave states would be located in the South
   (4) free states would have more land than slave states
   (5) eventually slavery would be allowed in all states if it were allowed to spread into new territories

Tip

It is important to know how to interpret common parts of maps such as these:
- The **title** that states the purpose of the map
- The **key** or **legend** that identifies the meaning of symbols on the map
- The **compass rose** that shows directions on a map
- Lines of **longitude** that show the distance east or west of the Prime Meridian
- Lines of **latitude** that show the distance north and south of the Equator

Question 3 refers to the following map and passage.

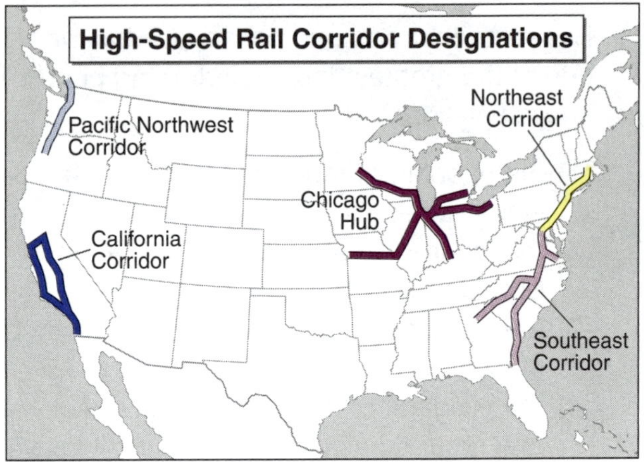

Source: Federal Railroad Administration, U.S. Department of Transportation

In the past few years, more and more people have become interested in High-Speed Rail (HSR) service in the United States. HSR would substantially reduce travel time between major cities along the corridors as indicated in the map. HSR corridors would help modernize train control systems, put into service new trains that could travel 100–150 miles per hour, be more environmentally friendly, and provide a cost-effective alternative to other types of transportation.

3. Based on the information the map and in the passage, why are there no plans for HSR corridors in the central United States?

   (1) HSR corridors must be located near large bodies of water, such as the Atlantic and Pacific Oceans.
   (2) HSR corridors are located in areas that have large populations, such as New York, Chicago, Seattle, and Los Angeles because they focus on transporting people from city to city.
   (3) HSR corridors would damage crops in states such as Kansas, Nebraska, and Iowa because of pollution caused by the trains.
   (4) HSR corridors cost too much money and so must be limited to the certain areas of the country.
   (5) HSR corridors must be tested first in large metropolitan areas before they can be set up in less populated areas.

Question 4 refers to the following map and passage.

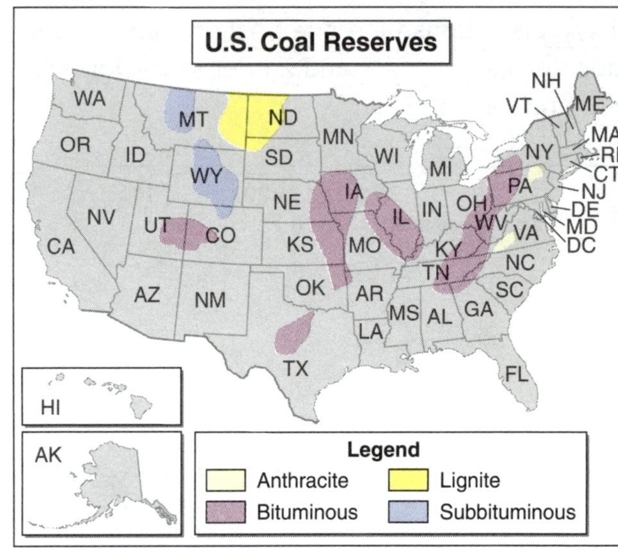

The United States has more coal reserves than any other country in the world. One-fourth of all known coal in the world is in the U.S. There are four types of coal mined in the U.S. today.

- Lignite—a soft, brownish-black coal that produces the least amount of heat
- Subbituminous—a dull black coal that gives off very little heat when it burns
- Bituminous—"soft coal" that produces more heat than Lignite or Subbituminous
- Anthracite—the hardest coal that produces the greatest amount of heat

Coal is used primarily to generate electricity. It is used to produce more than half of all the electricity used in the U.S.

4. Based on the map, which type of coal is found in the greatest abundance?

   (1) anthracite
   (2) bituminous
   (3) subbituminous
   (4) lignite
   (5) All are found in equal abundance.

Lesson 14

Maps
Maps in Science

Maps are used in science to provide many kinds of details in a way that makes information easier to understand. You can use maps to find out such things as the climate of an area, the physical features of the land, the natural resources in specific locations, or the distribution of wildlife.

The GED Science test will ask you to answer questions based on a variety of kinds of maps. Some questions will ask you to combine information from a map and a written passage to answer questions.

Try this GED example. Choose the <u>one best answer</u> to the question. Then check your answer.

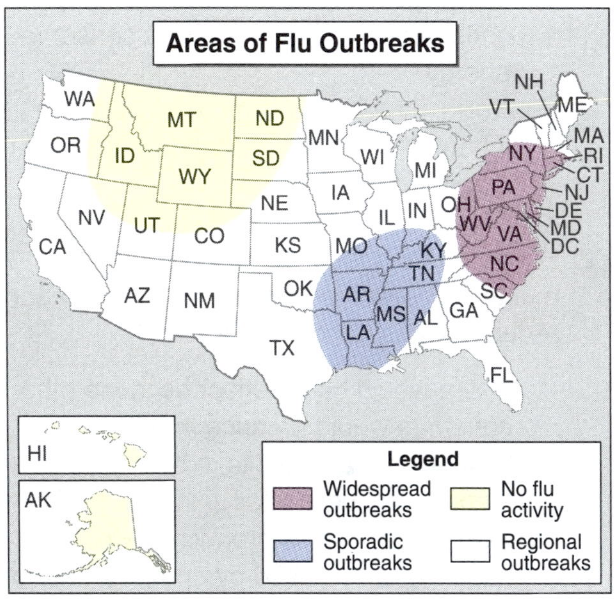

Each year, thousands of people get sick with influenza, or flu. A virus that attacks the respiratory system causes influenza. There are three types of flu virus: A, B, and C. Types A and B can be spread over a wide area. Type B usually causes fewer and less severe symptoms. Type C is very rare and causes the least symptoms of all.

Flu is spread through respiratory fluids that are present when you cough or sneeze. People can be contagious three to four days before their symptoms appear. The flu is usually spread in public places, such as schools or other facilities where many people gather. People take the flu home and spread it to their families. Sometimes the only way to stop the spread of the flu is to close schools or cancel public events, such as

meetings, ballgames, and other activities. This helps limit contact among people and reduces the likelihood of epidemic flu.

1. Based on the map and passage, why would widespread outbreaks of the flu be less likely to occur in an area such as Idaho?

   (1) The extreme winter weather acts as a barrier to germs, preventing the spread of flu.
   (2) Idaho has a relatively small population, thus less contact and exposure to the flu virus.
   (3) The people in Idaho have a healthier lifestyle than in other states.
   (4) People in Idaho are more likely to take the flu shot each year.
   (5) People in Idaho have a natural immunity to the flu virus.

---

1. **(2)** The population of Idaho is much smaller than that of states such as California. In many areas of Idaho, people live great distances from each other and may have limited opportunities to gather in public places where flu can be spread. The map and passage contain no information to support the other options.

Maps in Science

Directions: Choose the one best answer to each question. Questions 1 through 3 refer to the following maps and passage.

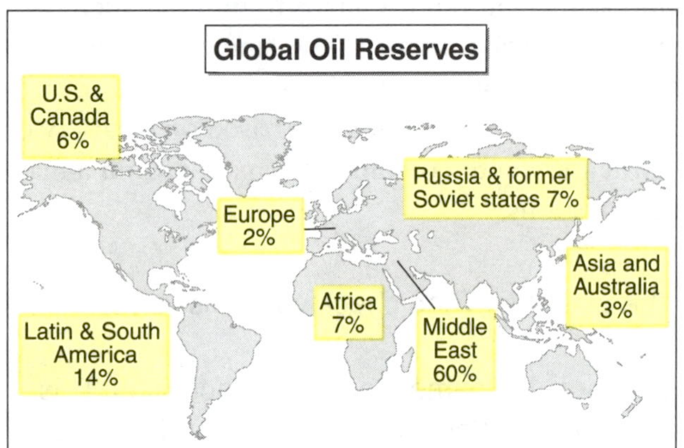

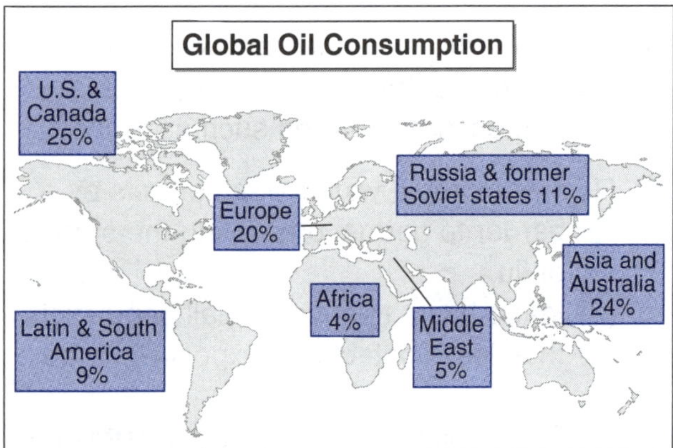

Although most people do not want to think about it, there are limited oil reserves in the world. People, especially those in more modernized areas of the world, continue to use oil and oil products at an ever-increasing rate. The largest oil reserves are in the Middle East, with Saudi Arabia having the largest of the reserves. Even though people from North America and Europe may wish to become less dependent on oil from the Middle East, the reality is that there are very limited oil reserves in other parts of the world.

Tip

Especially on maps where space is limited, a compass rose is frequently not included.

1. Based on the maps, which of the following most accurately reflects the level of oil consumption in North America compared to the rest of the world?

   (1) North America uses approximately the same amount of oil as the rest of the world.
   (2) North America consumes less than other modernized areas of the world.
   (3) North America consumes more than other larger and more populous areas of the world.
   (4) North America strictly limits its consumption of oil in order to conserve energy.
   (5) North America uses more oil because it has a higher population than the other areas of the world.

2. Based on the maps, what would be the most likely event to occur if the Middle East reduced its production of oil?

   (1) There would be no effect because other countries would produce more oil.
   (2) Latin America would take over as the leading producer of oil.
   (3) North American oil production would have to be increased by opening more oil wells in the Pacific and Atlantic Oceans.
   (4) Countries around the world would have to reduce their consumption of oil because there are not adequate resources available to make up for the shortfall.
   (5) Other countries would have to cut their use of oil so there would be enough for North America.

3. Based on the first map, the Middle East has the largest oil reserves in the world. Which part of the world has the second largest oil reserves?

   (1) Asia and Australia
   (2) North America
   (3) Africa
   (4) Europe and Russia
   (5) Latin and South America

Hurricane Tracks for 1994

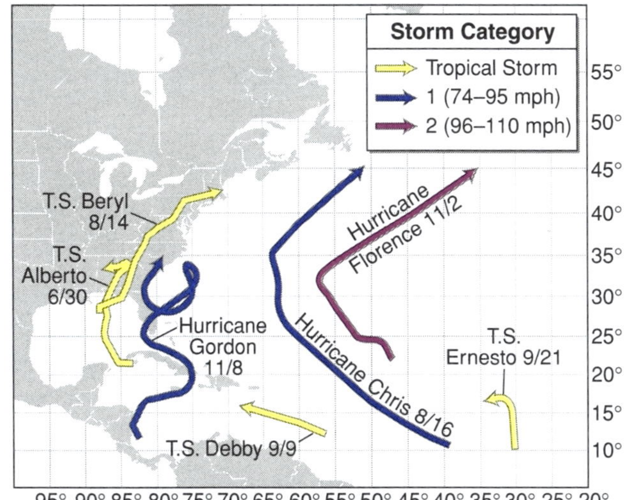

Tropical cyclones, or hurricanes, generally form in the Atlantic during the months of June through November. In June and July, tropical storms or hurricanes most often form in the Gulf of Mexico or Caribbean where the conditions are more favorable for development. August and September are usually the most active months for tropical storms and hurricanes forming in the Atlantic Ocean. These storms normally develop off the coast of Africa near the Cape Verde Islands. As the Atlantic waters cool, attention shifts back to the Caribbean and the Gulf of Mexico where storms develop in October and November.

Not all tropical storms or hurricanes strike the continental United States. Many of these storms are affected by wind shear, high winds from the northeast that cause the storms to either fall apart or to veer away from land.

4. Based on the map and passage, which of the following tropical storms or hurricanes did not form in an area and at the time of year in which it was expected?

(1) Alberto
(2) Ernesto
(3) Chris
(4) Debby
(5) Florence

5. The year 1994 was considered to be moderately active for tropical storms and hurricanes. However, only three storms made landfall in the continental U.S. that year. What is one explanation for the lack of landfall by the other storms?

(1) The storms were very strong.
(2) Upper level wind currents steered the storms away from land.
(3) The eye of the storm was too small to permit adequate development.
(4) The storm developed too far north to have an impact on the U.S.
(5) The ocean temperature was not high enough to support the storms.

6. If Tropical Storm Debby had sustained her strength and maintained her track, where would she most likely have made landfall?

(1) Cuba
(2) Mexico
(3) Florida
(4) Texas
(5) South America

7. Based on wind speed, which of the following storms would have caused the greatest damage if it had made landfall?

(1) Alberto
(2) Chris
(3) Debby
(4) Ernesto
(5) Florence

Tip

Maps usually have titles that give a general idea of the information included on the map. Maps can be large-scale, showing a small area of a state, country, or region with very specific details, or they can be small-scale, showing a larger area with less detail. Review the map scale to determine the type of detail you can expect on the map.

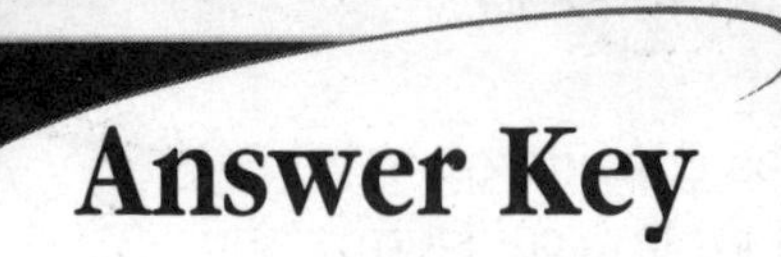

Answer Key

LESSON 1 (pages 4–5)
1. (2) 5. (3)
2. (1) 6. (1)
3. (2) 7. (1)
4. (4)

LESSON 2 (pages 7–8)
1. (3) 5. (1)
2. (1) 6. (4)
3. (2) 7. (1)
4. (4) 8. (1)

LESSON 3 (pages 10–11)
1. (4) 5. (4)
2. (5) 6. (3)
3. (1) 7. (5)
4. (1)

LESSON 4 (pages 13–14)
1. (5) 6. (3)
2. (3) 7. (1)
3. (5) 8. (4)
4. (2) 9. (3)
5. (2) 10. (4)

LESSON 5 (pages 16–17)
1. (1) 5. (5)
2. (2) 6. (2)
3. (4) 7. (3)
4. (4)

LESSON 6 (pages 19–20)
1. (2) 6. (3)
2. (3) 7. (5)
3. (3) 8. (5)
4. (3) 9. (3)
5. (2) 10. (3)

LESSON 7 (pages 22–23)
1. (5) 6. (2)
2. (3) 7. (2)
3. (4) 8. (3)
4. (2) 9. (3)
5. (4)

LESSON 8 (pages 25–26)
1. (2) 6. (5)
2. (2) 7. (5)
3. (3) 8. (3)
4. (4) 9. (3)
5. (1) 10. (3)

LESSON 9 (pages 28–29)
1. (1) 5. (4)
2. (4) 6. (1)
3. (2) 7. (1)
4. (3) 8. (4)

LESSON 10 (pages 31–32)
1. (5) 6. (3)
2. (2) 7. (1)
3. (4) 8. (2)
4. (5) 9. (5)
5. (1)

LESSON 11 (pages 34–35)
1. (5) 6. (4)
2. (3) 7. (4)
3. (3) 8. (2)
4. (5) 9. (1)
5. (5)

LESSON 12 (pages 37–38)
1. (1) 3. (1)
2. (3) 4. (4)

LESSON 13 (pages 40–41)
1. (4) 3. (2)
2. (2) 4. (4)

LESSON 14 (pages 43–44)
1. (4) 3. (2)
2. (2) 4. (2)

LESSON 15 (pages 46–47)
1. (3) 5. (2)
2. (4) 6. (2)
3. (5) 7. (5)
4. (5)

ACKNOWLEDGMENTS

This page constitutes an extension of the copyright page.

Grateful acknowledgment is made to the following authors, agents and publishers for permission to use copyrighted materials. Every effort has been made to trace the ownership of all copyrighted material and to secure the necessary permission to reprint. We express regret in advance for any error or omission. Any oversight will be acknowledged in future printings.

P.3,4,5 ©Courtesy of Library of Congress; p.6 ©Brumsic Brandon Jr., Courtesy of Florida Today; p.7a ©Doug Regalia; p.7b ©Neil Grahame, Courtesy of Spencer Newspapers; p.8a ©Chan Lowe/Tribune Media Services; p.8b ©Jeff MacNelly/Tribune Media Services. Additional photography from the Steck-Vaughn Collection.

APEX
TP_CF

9780739857472

76524047 – 29